PRAISE FOR *AIMING HIGH*

Evan Robb's deep belief in students and teachers shines through a spirit of unwavering comm ̄ ̄ ̄ ̄ ̄ ̄ ̄ ̄ ̄ ̄ ̄ ̄ ̄ver-
sation in honor of learning ̄ ̄ ̄ ̄ ̄ ̄ ̄ ̄ ̄ ̄ ̄ming
High envisions a broader pur ̄ ̄ ̄ ̄ ̄ ̄ ̄ ̄ ̄ared
leadership forms a foundatic ̄ ̄ ̄ ̄ ̄ ̄ ̄ ̄ce.
—Mary H ̄ ̄ ̄ ̄ ̄ ̄ ̄ ̄ing:
Foc ̄ ̄ ̄ ̄ ̄ ̄ ̄ ̄*Work That Matters*

Evan Robb not only aims high, but he also hits the mark on leadership in schools. Robb shares easy-to-use strategies and actions for all educators to use to better serve students and the school community while building a collaborative school culture. I am a better leader because of this book!
—Andrew Marotta, Principal, Leader, Author, Speaker
Leader of the #survivethrive movement
@andrewmarotta21
Milford, PA

Evan Robb provides school leaders with a pathway to improve student-centered learning by empowering all teachers to provide highly effective instruction and all students to embrace a culture of learning. Affirming, challenging, and timely!
—Chris Quinn, Retired District Leader, Classroom Teacher
London, Ontario, Canada

This book will equip educational leaders to empower staff through collaborative conversations and professional learning. If you are concerned about the detrimental effects of COVID-19 and want to use this moment to shake up learning, this is the book for you!
—Kasey Bell, Author, Podcaster, Blogger, Teacher
ShakeUpLearning.com
Celina, TX

Evan Robb has written a must-read primer for anyone in the K–12 education field. Robb sets the stage for the leadership needed in the community, for building relationships, and in literacy and math instruction.

—William D. Sroufe, Division Superintendent
Colonial Heights Public Schools
Colonial Heights, VA

Aiming High provides a structure for collaboratively creating a learner-focused culture. Evan Robb's experiences as a middle school principal provide implementation considerations guided by lessons learned, quotations, tips, and questions.

—Erik Youngman, Director of Curriculum,
Instruction, and Assessment
Libertyville District 70
Libertyville, IL

Both new and veteran educators will find that this book is the blueprint for creating future change and impact. It's time to lift our eyes and our minds and set our sights on *Aiming High* as we inspire students and our communities and cultivate a passion for learning.

—Vernon Wright, Speaker, Consultant, Leader, Author
Zero Apology Zone
Dallas-Ft. Worth, TX

I think we are all "pandemic-ed out," but Evan Robb's book will prepare all leaders during and after our next crisis or calm. This book should be added to your shelf, as it prepares you for nothing other than thoughtful, intentional leadership.

—Rick Jetter, Co-Founder
Pushing Boundaries Consulting
Creator of the #100StopSeries

Evan Robb highlights important and necessary leadership skills for maintaining a culture focused on learning during challenging times. This book provides education leaders with both practical and helpful strategies for ensuring learning gains for each and that every student stays at the center of our work.

—Randy L. Russell, Superintendent
Freeman School District
Freeman, WA

Aiming High deeply resonates with those wishing to reinfuse meaningful teaching and learning back into K–12 education and has my highest recommendation for low-burden, high-impact professional learning!

—Hans Appel, Educator, Speaker, Author, *Award-Winning Culture:*
Building Whole-Child Intentionality and Action Through Character,
Excellence, and Community

This book is packed with actionable strategies and ideas for making school a better place for teachers to teach and students to learn. This is truly a powerful book and one that I am sure principals and school leaders will keep front and center on their desks. Bravo!

—Timothy Rasinski, Professor of Literacy Education
Rebecca Tolle and Burton W. Gorman
Chair in Educational Leadership
Kent State University

This book is a practical and invaluable guide for school leaders, teachers, and staff who want students to succeed and develop a commitment to lifelong learning.

—Danny Brassell, Internationally Acclaimed Speaker, Author
Co-Creator of thereadinghabit.com

Evan Robb models the power of listening and embodies collaboration in developing a framework for literacy education. He examines a list of common ineffective literacy practices and offers a focus on four instructional practices and shares suggestions for professional learning and community involvement.

—Lester Laminack, Professor Emeritus
Western Carolina University
Whittier, NC

With a "students first" mindset, Evan Robb provides leadership tips that are logical and relevant to our work. With a "teachers first" mindset, he conveys the importance of acknowledging where individuals are and how to move them forward. Throughout this book, you will learn or reaffirm processes designed to make improvements with experience, learning, achievement, and empowerment in your school.

—Christopher Starczewski, Principal
Dudley Middle School
Dudley, MA

Aiming High cements Evan Robb as one of today's most relevant educational voices. Robb provides his readers with a vision and action steps for what schools can and should be. Whether you are an administrator or a teacher, this is a must-have resource!

—Kris Felicello, Superintendent of Schools
North Rockland Central Schools
Garnerville, NY

In this book, Evan Robb reasons that school leaders can improve instruction and learning in a culture of equity, student agency, and high expectations. In an age of electronic tools, Robb artfully argues that books, self-selected by students, are the windows through which learners can gain access and equity and see a vision of their future selves.

—Jeff Ikler, Director
Quetico Career and Leadership Coaching
Forest Hills, NY

Principal Evan Robb delivers once again. *Aiming High* is a strategic resource for building a rock-solid foundation to move any school out of the pandemic and into the future. You will continuously reference this book as you enhance a positive culture of learning within your school.

—Dean W. Packard, Principal
Charlton Middle School
Co-Host of @UnlockTheMiddle
Charlton, MA

Aiming High helps leaders understand how to work collaboratively to ensure a smooth-running school. Not only is there a focus on effective leadership, but the book also explores how to develop cooperative environments that support numeracy and literacy. Evan Robb aids leaders in creating an equitable learning culture that best helps all students succeed.

—Starr Sackstein, Chief Operating Officer, Mastery Portfolio
Author, *Assessing With Respect*
New York, NY

Author and principal Evan Robb demonstrates how to lead in today's complex world of education. His comprehensive approach dives into the essential competencies of leading a learning community. Thank you, Evan, for this important volume!

—Maribeth Edmunds, Principal
Monmouth Junction Elementary School
Monmouth Junction, NJ

This is an insightful guide for leaders on building trusting relationships, collaboration, equity, and accessibility to enhance student learning and school culture. If you are looking to instill a commitment to lifelong learning, this book will provide newfound inspiration.

—Joshua Stamper, Administrator
Author, *Aspire to Lead*
Teach Better Podcast Network Manager
Frisco, TX

This is essential reading for any leader who wants to move beyond mission statements and initiatives to shared, collective, and collaborative leadership that empowers. Whether you're a principal, coordinator, or team leader, you'll find a powerful and practical guide to cultivating an active, living culture of learning at your school.

—Tonya Gilchrist, Senior Literacy Strategist
Erin Kent Consulting
Middletown, VA

Equal parts practical and philosophical, this is a master class in how to build a collaborative, engaged, thoughtful, and equitable building and a curriculum and culture that will inspire both staff and students alike.

—Matthew Johnson, Language Arts Teacher
Author, *Flash Feedback: Responding to Student Writing Better and Faster—Without Burning Out*
Ann Arbor, MI

Aiming High provides readers with a pathway for understanding no matter where they fall on a school site level. It serves as an important part of any school's must-have collection.

—Jeff Kubiak, Educator, Author
Davis, CA

Aiming High

With love for Amelia and Liam, Lucas and Helena

Aiming High

Leadership Actions to Increase Learning Gains

Evan Robb

FOR INFORMATION:

Corwin
A SAGE Company
2455 Teller Road
Thousand Oaks, California 91320
(800) 233-9936
www.corwin.com

SAGE Publications Ltd.
1 Oliver's Yard
55 City Road
London EC1Y 1SP
United Kingdom

SAGE Publications India Pvt. Ltd.
B 1/I 1 Mohan Cooperative Industrial Area
Mathura Road, New Delhi 110 044
India

SAGE Publications Asia-Pacific Pte. Ltd.
18 Cross Street #10-10/11/12
China Square Central
Singapore 048423

President: Mike Soules
Associate Vice President and Editorial
    Director: Monica Eckman
Senior Acquisitions Editor: Ariel Curry
Senior Content Development Editor:
    Desirée A. Bartlett
Senior Editorial Assistant: Caroline
    Timmings
Production Editor: Melanie Birdsall
Copy Editor: Exeter Premedia Services
Typesetter: Exeter Premedia Services
Proofreader: Caryne Brown
Cover Designer: Gail Buschman
Marketing Manager: Morgan Fox

Printed in Canada

Library of Congress Cataloging-in-Publication Data

Names: Robb, Evan, author.
Title: Aiming high : leadership actions to increase learning
    gains / Evan Robb.
Description: Thousand Oaks, California : Corwin, 2022.
    | Includes bibliographical references and index.
Identifiers: LCCN 2021042046 (print) | LCCN 2021042047
    (ebook) | ISBN 9781071852910 (paperback) | ISBN
    9781071862131 (ebook)
Subjects: LCSH: Educational leadership—United States.
    | Academic achievement—United States. | School improve-
    ment programs—United States. | Literacy. | Numeracy.
Classification: LCC LB2805 .R64 2022 (print) | LCC LB2805
    (ebook) | DDC 371.2/011—dc23
LC record available at https://lccn.loc.gov/2021042046
LC ebook record available at https://lccn.loc.gov/2021042047

This book is printed on acid-free paper.

22 23 24 25 26 10 9 8 7 6 5 4 3 2 1

Contents

Acknowledgments

My thanks to all the administrators and teachers I've worked with throughout my career, for our interactions and conversations have caused me to reflect deeply on leadership as well as teaching and learning. It's been a delight to work with Ariel Curry, who has supported me throughout the planning and writing process with excellent suggestions, always responding quickly to my queries. Special thanks go to my mother, Laura Robb. She became my sounding board, and our discussions about topics and issues addressed in *Aiming High* enabled me to clarify my thinking as each chapter unfolded. To all the students I've taught and interacted with as their teacher, coach, and principal, sincere thanks for highlighting the need for differentiating instruction and equal access to the finest books and materials.

* * *

Author's Note: Names in the literacy snapshots that open each chapter are pseudonyms.

About the Author

 **Evan Robb** is presently principal of Johnson-Williams Middle School in Berryville, Virginia. He has served for more than twenty years as a building-level principal. Prior to being a school principal, he was an English teacher, department chair, and assistant principal. Evan is a recipient of the Horace Mann Educator of the Year Award. In addition, the NCTE Commission on Reading selected him to serve on its national board.

A TEDx speaker, Evan presents inspirational keynotes, workshops, and webinars on leadership, mindset, culture, impactful change, and how to improve literacy in schools. Evan has shared his ideas with thousands of educators at workshops across the United States and in other countries.

His first book, *The Principal's Leadership Sourcebook: Practices, Tools, and Strategies for Building a Thriving School Community*, was published by Scholastic in the fall of 2007. His next book, *The Ten-Minute Principal*, was published by Corwin in May 2019. Evan Robb and Laura Robb collaborated with Dave Burgess Publishing to write *TeamMakers*, published in August 2019. In addition, Evan partnered with Laura Robb to write *A School Full of Readers*, with Benchmark Education, published in January 2020.

Evan has been named one of the top twenty-five educational leaders to follow on Twitter. Scholastic EDU also named Evan one of the ten educators to follow on Twitter. Evan was recently named one of the ten most inspiring global thought leaders for 2020.

Introduction

I am an educator. I am a teacher. I am a middle school principal.

In early February 2020, I thought, based on my experiences, that I had seen it all. Then March came. March introduced us all to COVID-19; it changed our world. A global pandemic ignited swift moves by school divisions across the country and globe to close in-person school and shift to a new concept: emergency remote learning. Some schools suspended learning altogether. Those that remained open used virtual learning through the spring and often struggled as they tried to continue learning in unpredictable circumstances.

Just like you, I had never experienced a pandemic, nor was I aware of how changes would impact me personally, as well as teachers, staff, students, and families. Leading through this time has taught me much about flexibility, teamwork, and creating conditions for maintaining a culture focused on learning during challenging times. And we are indeed living in times of great challenges. Schools are transitioning back to a new normal, and your leadership is critical as schools create priorities for learning.

I don't have all the answers. However, I have learned that collaboration, active listening, and reflection can lead to changes that benefit teaching and students' learning. This book will guide you and other educational leaders working to transition your schools to a new normal for teachers, students, staff, parents, communities, and our nation.

IT'S TIME TO BEGIN!

There are two basic premises within this book that I will circle back to frequently:

- School leaders, teachers, and staff want students to succeed and develop a commitment to lifelong learning.

- The leader intentionally and collaboratively creates the conditions for improving learning through creativity and empowerment, leading to effective instruction that benefits all students and teachers.

As you read the two premises, you may also agree that no one goes into our profession expecting failure or mediocrity for students or themselves. Your belief that a leader and team of focused, committed educators can make a difference for each student in your school and schools across the globe should be your beacon. Your commitment to leadership, efficacy, optimism, faith, hope, and your school's mission can develop a productive and successful school community. But you face challenges daily—challenges that raise questions about whether you're providing enough support for teachers and students. Moreover, if effective leadership matters, then you'll collaborate with teachers to create the conditions that enhance students' learning gains.

During the next few years and beyond, improving all students' learning will be your top priority. *Aiming High* presents a framework for meeting the challenges you face today and into the future. In addition, *Aiming High* addresses the learning shortfalls that occurred among many students during COVID-19 due to not attending school, the inability to access the Internet, and consistently having the use of a computer or handheld device.

As you collaborate with teachers to understand students' social and emotional needs, you'll generate possible supports and create a path forward that works. You can read *Aiming High* to explore and develop the skills and intentions needed right now to collaboratively create the conditions and path to improve learning through creativity, innovation, and empowerment. As your school's leader, you can create or inhibit the conditions leading to effective instruction and a culture that benefits all students and teachers. This book provides a road map for developing a positive, trusting environment by collaborating with teachers and focuses your leadership on learning and growth for all.

In *Aiming High*, I will present a chapter-by-chapter pathway for you to empower teachers, students, and staff; build a learner-focused culture; and enhance trusting relationships. *Aiming High* has tips in each chapter addressing challenges and also includes suggestions if your school is hybrid. Chapters show you how to create the conditions leading to a culture where learning is a priority for all students.

I hope this book will affirm many of your beliefs, introduce you to new ideas and suggestions, and bring positive changes to your school community. It's time to start the journey dedicated to creating the conditions needed to enhance your school's culture and learning now and into the future.

SNAPSHOTS OF CHAPTERS 1 TO 8

I've organized *Aiming High* so you can easily access information. You can read the book from cover to cover or go to specific sections in each chapter based on your needs or interests. Chapters close with tips within for addressing the challenges and opportunities of hybrid learning leadership as well as a list of "actions" you can take.

Chapter 1: Redefining Instructional Leadership

The five goals of instructional leadership in this chapter reflect a shift from top-down to collaborative leadership. You'll also deepen your understanding of collaborative schoolwide initiatives and reflect on initiative overload and how to avoid it. The importance of pausing to assess whether initiatives are working will also be discussed.

Chapter 2: Collaborative Leadership: Activate, Influence, and Elevate

Everyone is better than anyone! In this chapter, you explore collaborative leadership and how you can work with staff and students to empower teacher and student leadership. You'll also learn how to create the conditions that affect your school's culture and students' learning gains.

Chapter 3: Building Trusting Relationships

The foundations of an effective school are trust and relationships. In this chapter, you can explore suggestions for building trust and positive relationships as well as how and why both can improve teaching and learning. Also discussed will be social and emotional and self-care needs—essentials for students' and staff's well-being.

Chapter 4: Supporting Students and Staff Through Professional Learning

Learn how to create, source, and organize professional development to build your teachers' capacity and enhance learning for all students. You can explore how to work collaboratively with your team to focus on professional development needs right now and how to meet all students' needs.

Chapter 5: Creating a Culture of Access, Equity, and High Expectations

Does your school have a culture of high expectations for students and staff? Expectations, personal efficacy, collective efficacy, and belief that students can learn and progress can help teachers move toward a student-centered learning approach. You'll also learn strategies for increasing access to materials, equity, and opportunities for students to grow.

Chapter 6: Leading for Literacy

Are you a reading principal? Do you champion literacy for all? Improving literacy in schools has always been important. This chapter provides actionable information and strategies you can use to support, enhance, and extend literacy in your building. Be the leader who promotes reading within your school, cultural sensitivity and empathy, and independent reading as you work toward creating a culture of reading.

Chapter 7: Leading for Numeracy

You can explore ideas and strategies for supporting numeracy in your school! Promote and collaboratively guide a numeracy program to meet every learner's needs. You'll see how to reach out to families and promote numeracy and review schedule changes that can add extra time for intervention and enrichment.

Chapter 8: Next Steps: Leading a Culture of Learning

Ultimately, all leaders want to establish a culture of learning. This final chapter offers ideas and strategies to fine-tune and enhance the conditions for improving students' literacy and numeracy as your school shifts toward a culture of learning. Chapter 8 will offer strategies and guidelines that can prepare you for the journey ahead!

CHAPTER 1

Redefining Instructional Leadership

My first job as the principal was opening a new junior high school. My goal was to lead a school where teachers and students looked forward to learning together every day—a school where teachers could meet the needs of every student. Moreover, I believed that to create a positive school culture, the assistant principal Joe Landers and I needed to know the content of all subjects taught as well as the state standards for each subject.

During the second week of school, I walked into Joe's office to discuss bus and lunch duty schedules and found him practicing Spanish using an online program. I asked, "Why are you trying to learn Spanish?"

He quickly responded, "You know the push in the building from you is all about instructional leadership and knowing the content of classes. I'm going to have to evaluate foreign language classes. Since I don't know any foreign languages, I decided to learn Spanish." I can vividly recall my reactions to Joe's explanation: overwhelmed, sweaty hands, not knowing how to respond immediately, and then seriously starting to question the goal I had established.

In a flash, I recognized the burden of knowing the content and curriculum standards of each subject taught!

The next day Joe and I had a long discussion, and we concluded that an administrative team could understand and evaluate course content and instruction by reading professional books and articles—learning the research. In addition, we eventually recognized the importance of cultivating trusting relationships with teachers, staff, and students. Trusting relationships allowed us to offer supportive feedback and carefully listen to teachers' ideas. I scheduled meetings for departments to have collaborative conversations focusing on instruction and how teachers could team up to improve their practice and learn from one another. Either Joe or I attended each meeting. Now, teachers accepted some of the responsibility for instructional leadership and looked up to their colleagues for suggestions and support—not only to Joe and me.

SHARING INSTRUCTIONAL LEADERSHIP

My first year as the principal pushed me to rethink an assumption I had embraced: instructional leadership was my job, and the assistant principal should also support this work. Beliefs change, and after many discussions with faculty during our second year at the junior high school, Joe and I recognized that schools could have many leaders and that administrators can and should create an environment for staff to grow as instructional leaders. No doubt, instructional leadership is hard work, but it is the work that holds the potential of supporting every learner in a school.

The principal's job is complex and often taxing. The duties that principals carried out, from my past experience, have not disappeared: bus, cafeteria, and hall duties, organizing initiatives and meetings, designing schedules, teacher evaluations, attending after-school events, addressing students' behavior issues, truancy, designing the school's budget, communicating with parents, and so on. With shared leadership, I serve as an instructional leader among teacher leaders. Today, especially during the pandemic and post-pandemic months when children return to learning in schools, sharing instructional leadership is a vital part of the principal's job more than ever.

At the most basic level, instructional leadership aims to improve student learning and teacher effectiveness. As a school leader, you should always focus your energy on developing the team and building their capacity to enhance teaching and learning. A daunting task, but one you can do!

RESEARCH SUPPORTS EFFECTIVE INSTRUCTIONAL LEADERS

Understanding and reflecting on research can help impact teaching and learning. The *Australian Professional Standard for Principals and the Leadership Profiles* (Australian Institute for Teaching and School Leadership) describes what effective administrators do:

> Principals create a positive culture of challenge and support, enabling effective teaching that promotes enthusiastic, independent learners committed to lifelong learning. Principals have a crucial responsibility for developing a culture of effective teaching, leading, designing, and managing the quality of teaching and learning and for students' achievement in all aspects of their development. They set high expectations for the whole school through

careful collaborative planning, monitoring, and reviewing learning effectiveness. Principals set high behavior and attendance standards, encouraging active engagement and a strong student voice.

APSPLP helps you better understand the characteristics of influential instructional leaders by defining the characteristics of effective leaders. As you review and reflect on the list below, highlight or underline the characteristics that define you and those you'd like to embrace.

- Holds high expectations
- Inspires others
- Uses data to enhance teaching and learning
- Focuses on improvement
- Models agency
- Builds connections and learning networks
- Commits to best practices and professional development
- Communicates effectively
- Models collaboration
- Encourages trust, creativity, and innovation

By reading and thinking about the characteristics of effective leaders, you can enhance your understanding of instructional leadership. However, these characteristics alone will not make you an effective instructional leader. What can result in more effective instructional leadership within your building depends on the level of shared leadership combined with knowledge and an understanding of the theory and research as well as what both look like in practice.

POSITIVE SHIFTS IN SCHOOL LEADERSHIP

Today, the school principal has many roles and responsibilities. I have seen a shift from top-down decision-making to leadership that focuses on empowering staff through collaborative conversations and professional learning. To become an effective principal, you must be an instructional leader intensely involved in curricular and teaching issues that directly affect student achievement (Cotton, 2003). In addition to sharing instructional leadership with faculty and staff, you are also a teacher, coach, mentor, connector, collaborator, communicator, and motivator. You can motivate teachers to move beyond a teacher-centered classroom and, with the support of ongoing professional learning, gradually shift to a student-centered approach. By disrupting traditional teaching practices, you enable teachers to address the specific learning needs of all children (Hallinger, 2005).

Post-pandemic school years in America and across the globe will be critical for you and other school leaders as you collaborate to identify how to support teachers and create classroom environments that enable students to make learning gains across the curriculum. There is an old saying: *we tend to get results where we put our time*. While redefining your role as an instructional leader who rallies staff around improving learning for every student, reflect on the five goals that follow along with the characteristics of effective leaders on pages 28–29.

FIVE GOALS THAT CAN REDEFINE YOUR INSTRUCTIONAL LEADERSHIP

Each goal has questions in italics for you to reflect on and can help you focus your instructional leadership on teaching and learning. As you consider your responses, think about the limited time you have each day and how specific goals can best increase learning for students and empower your team to embrace a student-centered approach.

1. BUILDING AND SUSTAINING YOUR SCHOOL'S VISION AND MISSION

To create a mission statement, you and staff need to have a collective vision of what's possible in a specific time frame, the challenges you'll meet and tackle, and the growth you hope to achieve—growth that affects teaching and learning. When you collaborate with staff to use their vision to develop a mission statement, they will be more committed to transforming the mission of improved learning into reality. Researchers point out that when you communicate to all stakeholders that learning is the school's most important mission, there's a strong likelihood that you will develop a high-achieving school (Cotton, 2003; Marzano et al., 2005).

Questions: *How does the staff's vision impact your mission statement? Who has created the mission statement? Does staff understand the vision and the mission? Each day, do you communicate the vision and mission through your words and actions?*

2. EFFECTIVE LEADERSHIP

Consider how you can delegate leadership work with clear expectations to other team members. Effective delegating builds agency and a capacity to learn and potentially frees you up to focus more on different aspects of school leadership. Principals who distribute leadership across their schools contribute to sustainable improvements within the school organization (Hargreaves & Fink, 2003).

Questions: *What are you delegating? How do you keep track of items and issues you delegate? How do you collect feedback from staff involved with shared leadership? What benefits do you see in sharing the leadership?*

3. LEADING A LEARNING COMMUNITY

Successful instructional leaders provide conditions through professional learning and collaborative conversations that incorporate the study of professional articles, books, and videos, successful curricula, hands-on demonstrations and practice of new skills, and peer coaching. To study the effect of new strategies on students' learning, school leaders use action research based on students' formative and summative data (Blasé & Blasé, 1999).

Questions: *How do you model agency for staff? How does staff know you're committed to student learning? How do you organize professional learning and collaborative conversations?*

4. DATA-BASED INSTRUCTIONAL DECISIONS

It is often said that schools are data-rich and action poor. Effective school leaders skillfully gather data and use it to determine instructional effectiveness. Data include different assessments but also provide a picture of the whole child using literacy stories, how peers view a student, and a student's words, actions, and behavior (Leithwood & Riel, 2003).

Questions: *How are you working with staff to ensure the data you have are what you need to inform decisions and take action? How do teachers keep records of and use formative assessment? Why is it important to know the whole child and not just data? What role do teachers have in organizing data for meetings to discuss students?*

5. MONITORING CURRICULUM AND INSTRUCTION

Trusting teachers to implement instruction effectively can increase their agency and self-efficacy, but you also need to monitor instruction with frequent classroom visits to verify the impact and results (Portin et al., 2003).

Questions: *How are you collaborating, observing, and providing feedback on the instructional curricula in your school? Are teachers moving to a student-centered approach? Do teams and departments discuss students' progress and collaborate to suggest interventions and support? How can you discover what professional development your team needs?*

At times, you might feel like a juggler—encouraging teamwork, using data and knowledge of the whole child to help teachers plan instruction and interventions, monitoring curriculum and instruction, and ensuring staff carry out their collaborative vision and mission—which can be daunting! Beware, however, that the desire to create and implement many changes at once can diminish the goal of enabling all students to improve and progress in all subjects.

SCHOOLWIDE INITIATIVES CAN IMPROVE INSTRUCTION AND LEARNING

Initiatives aimed at improving students' reading, writing, and numeracy work well when teachers and other staff members actively support them and have been part of the process from the start. However, though most schoolwide initiatives begin with positive goals, not all of them are successful. As you read on, you'll explore reasons that pinpoint why some schoolwide initiatives don't build forward momentum and often fail, as well as why some initiatives take hold and work.

INITIATIVE OVERLOAD

When I was a new principal, I thought it was best to develop and implement multiple initiatives at one time—the more the better. "Initiative frenzy" was a term my faculty used in jest as new initiatives were thrust upon them. At the start of a school year, and sometimes at multiple points during the year, they learned of a new initiative added to the always-expanding list. Launched by me as well as Central Office staff, new initiatives soon grew to unmanageable numbers, and many fizzled out and failed. Here is the big takeaway along with a question to reflect on and discuss with your administrative team:

- Working on seven or more initiatives is counterproductive, as it's impossible for you and staff to successfully implement all of them during a school year. Moreover, a staff's joking about "initiative frenzy" quickly sours and can transform into anger and frustration due to the amount of extra time they must invest to work on all initiatives. Eventually, as staff's commitment wanes, so do initiatives. *Why can initiative overload become a roadblock to effective leadership and change?*

Even if you have embraced the five goals and effective leadership characteristics, working on several major schoolwide initiatives at once can diminish your effectiveness as a leader. In addition, resist making top-down, solo decisions by choosing the initiative for your staff.

TOP-DOWN INITIATIVES

Though you might be tempted to make a top-down decision about adopting a schoolwide initiative, avoid the
temptation! A colleague, a high school principal, shared a
"great idea" for launching a schoolwide initiative. With no
input or feedback from faculty, he planned and approved
of a project-based learning (PBL) initiative! Teachers had
to read two articles (most knew nothing about PBL) on
PBL, create a new project-based unit every nine weeks,
and submit their plans and a rubric to the principal for
review. Resistance among faculty was palpable, and
when some teachers refused to fulfill his demands, his
top-down decisions became punitive: he documented
teachers and required they plan units under his supervision. As teacher resistance spread, the building's
culture shifted away from a school focused on teaching
and learning. Teachers who refused to comply with his
demands feared reprisals. Not wanting to be part of this
unhealthy environment, many teachers left. And to the
relief of remaining staff, the principal left, too. Here are
two takeaways and questions to discuss with your leadership team:

- The principal used positional authority to require
  teachers with limited knowledge and no experience
  design to implement PBL units each nine-week
  semester. He tried to enforce an initiative that was
  obviously unpopular among faculty. *What did this
  principal fail to do that's crucial to effective leadership?*

- Teachers will resist initiatives when the principal
  enforces them without buy-in or a thoughtful plan
  by refusing to develop unit plans and rubrics. Their
  criticisms of the principal's top-down decisions went
  underground. *What could a group of teachers have done to*

try to alter the principal's thinking and actions and possibly turn this initiative into a successful one?

PBL, an excellent way to motivate and engage students, did not flourish within the building. The principal used his positional authority to force teachers to comply. Great ideas are worthless if the team is unwilling to get on board. What he should have done was seek teachers' input using collaborative discussions to increase teachers' commitment to and investment in PBL.

COLLABORATIVE SCHOOLWIDE INITIATIVES

Staff will rally around a schoolwide initiative when you've taken the time to collaborate and build trusting relationships. When I had a personal goal of implementing a culture of reading in my school, I understood the importance of including teachers, our school librarian, and other staff in small-group conversations and planning sessions that I and other administrators attended. Teams and departments held meetings to create a list of what our middle school needed to put reading front and center in all subjects. Ms. Deem, our librarian, led a group of volunteers to study the school's library and develop a list of needs that would make the library the "family room" of our school—a place students would find inviting. A team of teachers studied the needs of building classroom libraries with books that represented the diverse cultures in our nation. Staff met to explore ways they could foster a love of reading among students. Groups recommended articles to study, videos to watch, and schools to visit. The entire school community worked in teams that reported their ideas at full faculty meetings.

Ms. Deem used this school initiative to enhance reading across our building. Teachers evaluated books' cultural relevance, and how much independent reading occurred in classes and in the school's library. Ms. Deem challenged staff to elevate independent reading of self-selected books for all students as we worked as a team toward a culture of reading within our building.

This initiative is in its fourth year, and issues of replacing books, estimating enough funding for purchases, and adding new books and materials to class and the school's library are ongoing. Follow-up years are not as intense as the first two years, but the point is that some initiatives are ongoing and will always benefit from adjusting and rethinking; adding one to two new initiatives to these is doable. Here are two takeaways and questions to discuss with your teachers and staff:

- Staff will rally around a schoolwide initiative when you've taken the time to collaborate and build trusting relationships. *Even if the process takes more time, why is it important to turn over the responsibility for developing a schoolwide initiative over to teachers and staff and put them in charge through collaborative groups?*

- School leaders must make an effort to participate in schoolwide initiatives. *Why is it beneficial for administrators to attend collaborative discussions as a group member?*

You can foster trust and cultivate relationships among teachers and students by making collaborative decisions that can lead teachers to learning about and trying current research-based instructional practices. Staff and students should always know the direction of the initiative as it moves forward and feel valued and trusted, so they take intentional risks to become better teachers and learners. Remember, when you encourage leadership among teachers, staff, and students, you're redefining your role as instructional leader and enabling your school community to see the relevance of the initiative to their learning and progress.

ASSESSING WHETHER INITIATIVES WORK

Several years ago, when staff and I developed initiatives for the next school year that included differentiation, using technology to enhance instruction, and innovation, most teachers raised questions about instruction as we sought to identify queries that could monitor students' learning and progress. Teacher collaboration resulted in four focus questions to spark ongoing conversations and bring even more in-depth instructional focus (DuFour et al., 2010). The four questions (see below) guided conversations across the school among guidance staff, administrators, and teachers. These conversations raised questions about helping students struggling academically and/or with peer relationships, how to better support learners' academic needs in classrooms, social-emotional needs, and family outreach. Groups shared their notes. Under each focus question, you'll find teachers' suggestions for assessing in italics.

FOUR FOCUS QUESTIONS

1. How do we know if students are learning?

   Confer, observe them while they work, read written work in journals, listen to conversations, take running records, and review and assess station work.

2. What do we do when students aren't successful?

   Target areas that need strengthening, plan interventions, confer, use the gradual release model, organize peer partnerships, reteach, notice, and share every small gain.

3. How do we respond when students are excelling with the curriculum?

   Ask them what they'd like to learn, offer choices for extending their learning, invite them to work with a partner or small group on a collaborative project, and explore how technology can support enrichment.

4. How are we using best practices and research as we plan and provide instruction?

   Grade-level teams or departments meet to share instructional practices and research behind them. Assess practices to ensure they help teachers meet all students' needs.

A high level of focus on students' learning in your school shines a spotlight on instruction and is important, but even more so during the COVID-19 pandemic, as you transition in the fall to more students returning to classrooms. Tap into the expertise and experiences of your administrative team, teachers, staff, and students—knowing that with their feedback and support you can create the conditions needed for learning to occur for every child. There are no quick fixes, but with teamwork you can find a positive pathway forward.

This book isn't a playbook that asks you to follow, in sequence, a series of guidelines.

The primary purpose of this book is to show how certain elements of leadership can equip you to effectively lead and empower your teachers as your school returns to normalcy after a year of COVID-19. You'll be able to select suggestions for improving literacy and numeracy in your school as well as review suggestions for productive collaboration with faculty, how to create shared teacher leadership, equity, and access, develop schoolwide initiatives, and build trusting relationships.

HYBRID LEADERSHIP TIPS

The characteristics of instructional leaders can be modeled through your words and actions. Ensure that you connect with your staff frequently. Connections are different during virtual and hybrid learning, but their value does not decrease. Video meetings are important because your team needs to hear you and see you. During face-to-face meetings your words and actions should model optimism. It can be difficult to maintain optimism during challenging times, but by noticing and noting positive actions and behaviors such as increased student attendance, uplifting student art projects, excellent feedback on curriculum, and so forth, you enable teachers to focus on what's working prior to addressing areas that require rethinking and extra work.

(Continued)

Keep your focus on teaching and learning. If your teachers feel overwhelmed and frustrated by technology, extend the same grace to them that you encourage your teachers to offer to students—then have your school's tech person support them. Initiatives can be collaboratively assessed using the four focus areas on pages 19 and 20 as discussion points. However, since virtual and concurrent teaching can be challenging and frustrating, gauge the pulse of your staff and start small.

Communicate to students and their families through video, news-letters, or virtual meetings. Consider starting or continuing a student advisory group, so that you stay connected with students, listen to their challenges, questions, and successes, bring these to teachers, and together find ways to provide support.

Set aside time to invest in your learning by chatting with area school leaders, watching videos and TEDx Talks, reading profes-sional articles and blogs, and taking time for self-care. Finding balance in your life and setting aside time to do what brings you joy will make you a more effective leader.

CONSIDER THESE ACTIONS AND AIM HIGH

Each chapter will end with a list of actions for you to consider as you redefine your role as the instructional leader of your school.

- Identify your strengths as an instructional leader and list a few areas you hope to improve.
- Collaborate with staff to decide on and prioritize possible initiatives.
- Empower teachers to determine professional learning needs and attend the sessions they organize.

- Invite staff to annually revisit your school's vision and mission to refine and adjust the content.

- Form a team of teachers across disciplines to recommend possible initiatives that can advance learning gains for all students.

- Generate ways with your administrative team that you can expand leadership among teachers, staff, and students and meet with groups to ask for volunteers.

- Gather data on a specific initiative and discuss its impact on students' learning.

- Ensure you've created an environment where teachers can risk trying new and innovative teaching practices.

Closing Reminder

Collaborating with teachers and staff to share instructional leadership and develop schoolwide initiatives that advance research-based instruction and students' learning create the conditions that enable everyone to fulfill your school's vision and mission.

CHAPTER 2

Collaborative Leadership

Activate, Influence, and Elevate

An interdependent vision can be realized only through collaborative action, so relationships at work become central" (Senge, 1994). This quote from Senge's *The Fifth Discipline Fieldbook* reminds me of the importance of collaboration and positive relationships with a team. I believe in collaboration and building trusting relationships, but in March 2020, COVID-19 challenged these educational beliefs.

The March 2020 initial planning meetings with my administrative team proved daunting and frustrating because of the pandemic. The team and I had many questions: *Where do we start? How is this going to work? How do we support teachers? How do we support students emotionally and academically? How will we adjust the ways we communicate with parents?* We faced an unexpected challenge, and I, for one, felt unprepared.

During the days of the pandemic that followed school closure, colleagues would frequently say, "We didn't go to graduate school to learn how to lead in a pandemic!" Again and again, I would hear similar complaints from them, sometimes in jest, other times in anger or frustration. Gradually, their words affected my mindset. I felt my situation was hopeless.

Throughout the day, questions bombarded my mind: *How could I support teachers and students? How could I keep our culture alive? How could I assure families we'd find ways to work with them and their children?* I felt that I couldn't tackle these changes alone or even with the help of my administrative team. However, the answer came to me when I was exercising on my stationary bike, a place where I think, gain clarity, and at times find answers to my questions. The answer was simple and clear. Source my teacher's expertise.

The next day I told my administrative team, "I have the answer. I understand how virtual learning can work! Here's what we're going to do. I'll begin the conversation in a video meeting with staff this way, 'I don't know a path forward; I don't have answers.'" I received perplexed looks, and as I started to explain, interruptions stalled my explanation.

"Evan, your great idea is you don't know what to do?"

I leaned back on my chair, "Yep, that's correct. We have smart teachers. If together, we source the expertise in our faculty, I'm certain that we can find a pathway."

The next day during our meeting, I activated teachers' thinking by inviting them to generate suggestions to support all of us as we moved rapidly from in-person to virtual learning. My administrative team and I spoke about our faculty's strength and how their ideas could influence developing guidelines to support each other as never before. I explained that I did not have the answers, and that like them, I worried about the uncertainty ahead. However, finding realistic solutions was my goal. I shared stories of how we, as a school, had always been innovative and creative and reminded teachers that I had faith that they were up to the pandemic's challenges. I scheduled a series of daily meetings with all the teachers and administrators to discuss the next steps. I closed the meeting by reiterating that our commitment as a community was to safety, students, and staff.

Over several meetings, a collaborative leadership team of grade-level team leaders and department chairs emerged. By working together, we learned about each other, grew closer, and created a virtual learning plan to positively impact teachers, staff, students, and families. Each meeting closed with my elevating and praising their efforts and thinking because they always showed me they were up to the task of meeting every challenge. I believed this, and over time they did, too.

Optimism is an important part of leadership and to maintain hope, I explained that the brightest, most able scientists in the world would be working together on a vaccine that would change our present situation. As I write this chapter, the world is vaccinating people at a level never before imagined.

Collaboration enables teams to tackle unexpected challenges head-on! Living through COVID-19 highlighted seven lessons I learned.

LESSONS LEARNED

- Source your team by tapping into each person's expertise and strength.

- Focus on your vision and goals as supports for making tough decisions.

- Search for ways to work with your leadership team and staff to find solutions. It is okay not to know the answers, and this should be the catalyst for collaboration.

- Flatten your organization and give everyone an opportunity to contribute as well as empower leadership.

- Build trusting relationships when working collaboratively to solve challenges.

- Believe in your team and always let them know why.

- Choose optimism, keep hope alive, and communicate that with teamwork better days are ahead.

The seven lessons strengthen collaboration and enable groups to risk sharing all ideas in order to prioritize those they feel might work.

COLLABORATION BUILDS COMMITMENT TO POSITIVE CHANGE

Collaboration encourages conversations that can lead to pedagogical change, allowing teachers' input to impact their instructional growth, your school's curriculum, and students' learning (Spillane et al., 2004). Moreover, the impact on students' learning and teacher growth benefits your school now and into the future because effective collaboration increases teachers' ownership of curricula changes and adjustments and also boosts their continual investment. You don't need to know all the answers, but by collaborating with your faculty, you will see that possible solutions to challenges will arise.

As the principal, you have the role of shaping the discussion, guiding your faculty, and creating the conditions for collaboration to occur (Mendel et al., 2002). This style of leadership allows you to be an active participant in decisions and to model the collaboration you would like at teacher and staff meetings and among students and teachers. I've developed five characteristics of effective collaborative leadership for you and your administrative team to reflect on and discuss.

FIVE CHARACTERISTICS OF EFFECTIVE COLLABORATORS

A purposeful goal to set is that you and your team continually model these traits during daily interactions with staff, students, and parents, allowing all stakeholders to experience them and ultimately include them as they interact with school community members.

1. **Be action-oriented:** Model that you view collaborating with staff to discuss problems and challenges as opportunities for teamwork that explores and discovers solutions.

2. **Be inclusive:** Seek opportunities to involve others in decisions to increase ownership and to demonstrate a commitment to a shared process.

3. **Show your beliefs:** Always communicate through your words and actions how much you value optimism, hope, and high expectations for students and staff.

4. **Strive to be a servant leader:** Every day show your commitment and dedication to members of your

school community by listening, increasing their self-confidence, and finding ways to support them.

5. **Cultivate patience:** By offering teachers and staff time to understand changes, challenges, and school initiatives, you model that growth is a process and not an event. Be an active listener who values and reflects on feedback from staff and students.

When your faculty observes, hears, and experiences you exhibiting the five characteristics of effective collaborators, your school culture can begin to shift to an increased focus on teaching and learning. As you consider being more collaborative to increase learning gains for all students in your school, remember that part of leadership is projecting your beliefs and being sincere. Remember, if the faculty perceives your actions or words as insincere, you cannot be effective.

LEADERSHIP TIP

How you work with your faculty will build bridges or walls. Be genuine, seek collaborative opportunities, and strive to have congruency between your words and actions. To lead the change, you need to model and be the change!

SEVEN CONDITIONS THAT FOSTER COLLABORATION

To collaborate with teachers and develop the shifts and changes that can lead to learning gains for every student, you'll want to continually assess whether the seven conditions that foster collaboration in your school are thriving. As you evaluate your schools' collaborative temperature, you'll find that teachers may be involved in some or all of the conditions that follow—your purpose is to strengthen each one through conversations, mentoring, modeling, and shining the spotlight on conditions that are flourishing in order to encourage all staff to embrace and lean into each one (Fairman & Mackenzie, 2012).

1. **Agency:** Initiate and seek opportunities to learn more about instruction and learning.

2. **Risk taking:** Intentionally build a community that values collaboration and trusting relationships, so that staff take risks and try new methods without the fear of administrative reprisal or personal failure. Help staff know that failures are opportunities to learn and improve.

3. **Positive interactions:** Encourage teamwork to generate ideas and problem-solve, as such interactions can improve professional agency, enhance trusting relationships, and boost staff morale.

4. **Advocacy:** When you build trust and relationships, you empower staff to have a voice, and advocacy increases. Be the leader who encourages teachers to be advocates for their students' needs, professional learning opportunities, curricula adjustments, classroom libraries, updating materials, and so on.

5. **School improvement:** Show staff how much you value their contributions, suggestions, feedback, and respect their voices, by noticing and noting what they do and say in a conversation or email. Staff that feels appreciated will more likely engage in school improvement and commit to important initiatives.

6. **Communication:** You can model timely communication by responding to staff's queries within 24 hours as well as create short videos for parents that celebrate teachers' efforts and students' progress. As you model the importance of communication, teachers will find effective ways to communicate with students and families.

7. **Networking:** Empower teachers and staff to network within and beyond their school community through social media and by arranging meetings to share ideas. You'll not only enhance learning and professionalism, but you can also strengthen self-efficacy as teachers and staff share literacy and numeracy stories with other educators and deepen their understanding of how and why they can impact students' learning.

A strong, focused collaborative faculty can accomplish the challenges of returning schools to a new normal, post-pandemic and beyond. Moreover, when instruction that supports learning gains for every student is a foundational belief, then monitoring students' progress becomes the way to support learners. A collaborative model allows you to become a learner among learners, creating opportunities for you to be involved and visible with instruction, curriculum, assessment, and professional learning as you model the behaviors needed for progress and success. Even though you work toward having your entire staff embrace instructional changes such as differentiation and blended learning, there will be resisters. Avoid ignoring them and hoping that they join the majority. Instead, listen to their objections, encourage them to read and discuss informative articles and watch videos, and suggest they pair up with a colleague for additional conversations. You can't force them to change, but you can create learning opportunities that can cause them to rethink their views.

As the principal, you influence the collaborative conditions in your school more than any other staff member. The seven conditions plus your encouragement can empower faculty to develop and lobby for leadership roles and bring substantive changes to instruction that elevates and honors students' progress with literacy and numeracy.

INTRODUCING SHARED INSTRUCTIONAL LEADERSHIP

To maintain the collaborative spirit you've developed and extend it to teacher leadership opportunities, you can call for volunteers to fill leadership roles you've identified, or you can encourage teachers to develop leadership roles based on specific, observable needs. It will take time to build a culture of shared instructional leadership and help staff view such roles as opportunities for growth instead of "more work."

Start conversations at team and department meetings and invite teachers to find articles on shared instructional leadership using a search engine and share them with colleagues and administrators. Once discussions of these articles begin, it's important for you to attend meetings, so you can gauge where teachers are with taking on leadership responsibilities, developing protocols for gaining approval, and communicating progress with you.

Steadily improving all students' gains in literacy and numeracy should be a primary goal of sharing instructional leadership.

GETTING STARTED WITH SHARED INSTRUCTIONAL LEADERSHIP

The focus of teacher leadership opportunities is to identify the needs of all students as they return to school and then determine the instructional moves and data that can lead to steady progress for each one. You can organize volunteers into cross-grade-level teams to explore a topic as well as find professional articles, books, and videos for study to increase teachers' understandings. You'll need to establish guidelines for the process with teachers, so you and your administrative team remain in the loop as the process moves forward:

- **Approving the topic:** This will occur when you and faculty collaborate and choose two to three topics to pursue.

- **Researching available materials:** The shared leadership team finds resources such as online professional articles, excerpts from books, and YouTube videos that can increase administrators' and teachers' knowledge of a specific topic.

- **Scheduling meetings, reading, and discussing:** The leadership team submits a schedule for meeting with an administrator to the principal for approval.

- **Sharing recommendations:** These can be shared with all staff and administrators in a shared folder the leadership team creates.

- **Moving to actionable steps:** Once the staff has read the recommendations, there should be collaborative discussions to evaluate the recommendations and explore costs for materials as well as teachers' reactions.

It's important that someone in the teacher leadership team jot down notes of key discussion points and recommendations in a shared computer folder. This allows members who attended the meetings to review and adjust their notes, but it also keeps you, faculty, and staff abreast of what's happening as long as the shared folder is accessible to everyone.

MOVING FORWARD WITH SHARED INSTRUCTIONAL LEADERSHIP

The list of possible topics that follows won't be implemented in one school year. Again, through collaborative discussions, decide on two to three areas of shared instructional leadership to work on—areas that everyone agrees will result in improved teaching and learning. You can invite teachers to add a new topic after one has been successfully implemented.

Review, reflect on, and collaboratively discuss the shared instructional leadership suggestions that follow and select two topics you and teachers believe are high priorities for your school. Since the list that follows is not exhaustive, your team might decide on other topics such as grading because they believe that when students receive low grades, their self-confidence and desire to work diminish and become roadblocks to improvement. Remember, the purpose of shared leadership initiatives relates to the overarching goal of this book: increasing *all* students' learning gains.

- **Develop culturally relevant and responsive teaching,** a research-based approach that invites teachers to make connections between students' learning in school and their cultures, languages, family traditions, and experiences. Connections engage students with the curriculum and bring relevance to materials and tasks.

- **Move to a student-centered approach** that includes students' choices and collaborative discussions and projects to motivate and engage students in meaningful work.

- **Focus on access and equity** to meet all students' learning needs by ensuring there are books and materials that meet the diverse learning levels in classes as well as classroom libraries with culturally relevant books students can see themselves in as well as use them to learn about other cultures and lifestyles.

- **Use assessments to guide instruction** so that teachers continually monitor students' progress to support them as well as make teaching and learning decisions.

- **Acting as advocates for students' needs** invites teachers to lobby for students who require additional support or a series of interventions to improve.

- **Make independent reading happen** by helping faculty understand how daily reading of self-selected books is the practice students need to improve their skill. Also important is to investigate teachers' schedules to ensure that independent reading can occur when classes meet.

- **Integrate station learning,** a strategy that allows teachers to differentiate by supporting a group of students who require additional practice in English Language Arts classes and other content subjects. while others work at enrichment or reinforcement stations. This type of differentiated scaffolding and support can be used by teachers from kindergarten to Grade 12.

- **Embrace differentiation** to find ways to help children at different instructional reading levels actively learn from materials they can read. Teachers also adjust process and expectations and what students create to demonstrate learning.

- **Mentor new teachers** to reduce stress, and have new teachers regularly meet with a mentor throughout the year to acclimate them to the school's culture, expectations for teachers, deadline dates for reports, and so on. In other words, by reducing the stress created by not knowing and making mistakes, new teachers can focus their energy on instruction and students' learning.

- **Consider personalized learning** by developing learning experiences for individuals tailored specifically for their needs and providing choices for students among a set of activities. Personalized learning builds on students' strengths and can enable learners to meet goals.

- **Use choice boards** to enhance students' engagement and motivation to learn by offering them a choice of activities to boost their learning of a concept, applying a strategy, or solving problems.

As you encourage staff to collaborate to select, research, and then put into action shared instructional leadership projects that matter to your school's teaching and learning, students will experience success.

RETURNING TO A NORMAL SCHOOL DAY

As your school returns to a normal day, it's vital for you to work with your faculty and staff to focus on culture building, instruction, learning, and elevating your faculty's capacity to influence children's learning. Being specific and targeted is the way to move ahead. Many schools had a halt to professional development during the pandemic. At times, a lull in professional growth can encourage staff to revert to prior methods that may be comforting during a turbulent time but may not be effective for students.

When your school reopens, you have a professional responsibility to refocus instruction and students' learning and growth. The most significant influence on students' learning progress is highly expert, inspired, passionate teachers and school leaders working to maximize the learning gains of all students in their care (Hattie, 2015). You have the key role in helping your faculty find and harness their energy, passion, and drive for supporting all students. The five tips that follow can help you focus priorities and initiatives and can increase the likelihood of success for you, your faculty, and students.

SUCCESS TIPS YOU CAN CONTROL

Collaborate with teachers and discuss the tips that follow so they understand the thinking behind your recommendations.

- **Start small** and avoid overwhelming yourself and teachers.
- **Communicate** to your faculty frequently and with specific purposes and information.
- **Form partnerships** by collaborating with your faculty and staff.
- **Choose optimism** and emphasize what's working.
- **Cultivate and model collective efficacy** so your entire school community believes that with hard work everyone can move forward.

Harnessing the intellect on your faculty and staff, collaborating, and then empowering them to lead can help you meet the challenges of leading when students return to school after the pandemic and beyond. Collaborations, partnerships, and school-focused initiatives can sustain learning over time as you focus everyone on long-term gains instead of short-term quick fixes.

HYBRID/VIRTUAL TIPS

Leadership can exist and thrive virtually or with a hybrid school schedule.

Communication

Always essential and even more so if disconnected from staff.

Tip: Arrange scheduled opportunities to speak with your entire staff and groups, such as grade-level teams and departments. Work with teams and departments to establish scheduled meetings focused on students and their progress as well as sharing ideas and interventions to meet the needs of striving readers.

Collaboration

Virtual leadership and teaching can be great opportunities for collaboration.

Tip: Use video meetings on your platform of choice to collaborate and problem-solve with your team. Set the purpose of meeting, encourage discussion, value ideas, and demonstrate how the collaboration you and your team are doing is making a difference.

Teachers' Roles

Empower teachers to have leadership opportunities in a virtual environment.

Tip: The collaboratively developed initiatives for your school are leadership opportunities for staff. Empower staff to create goals based on your school's initiatives and to share updates on successes and challenges.

As you and teachers collaborate to develop shared instructional leadership opportunities, expect a few failures and/or less-than-stellar results. When you view these as opportunities to learn and try again, you send a powerful message to staff, teachers, and students: taking risks can result in failures, and that's okay as long as you see failures as information to help teaching and learning improve and revise plans so that progress occurs. Much of what I have communicated to you centers on your role to model and change. Here's the message to communicate: there is no shame in failing as long as you use failures to learn and then redirect your efforts toward success.

CONSIDER THESE ACTIONS AND AIM HIGH

- Meet with staff to review present schoolwide initiatives and suggest one to two new ones to explore.
- Collaborate with faculty and staff and determine one to two initiatives that would improve instruction and students' learning.

- Invite faculty and staff to collaborate and develop a set of shared instructional leadership possibilities. Then, collaborate with groups to explore shared leadership ideas that can enable all students to make significant learning gains.

- Create a cross-grade-level team to look at professional learning that reflects teachers' needs and desire to grow. Then, collaborate with faculty to set priorities and decide which ideas teacher leaders could develop and help implement.

- Examine the level of risk taking you and your administrative team encourage among staff to identify ways to encourage staff to try new instructional practices.

- Invite grade-level teams to collaborate and examine your communication with all school community stakeholders and then create a list of recommendations for you to review and discuss further.

- Reflect on how you positively impact your school's climate, culture, and the professional attitude of teachers and then jot down areas that affect student learning—areas you believe require more attention. Implement them and gather feedback from teachers as you place students' progress at the center of your agenda.

- Notice whether teachers are taking risks by trying new instructional practices that reach and improve all learners. Always assure faculty that it's okay for a lesson not to work when they first use it, but that you want them to view missing the mark or failing as an opportunity to learn and try again.

Closing Reminder

Maintaining a collaborative school environment ensures that you and staff are a team working on students' progress, curricula changes and adjustments, and shared leadership through communication that values your team's input and feedback.

CHAPTER 3

Building Trusting Relationships

John was starting his fourth year as a principal. Students and staff enjoyed the school, and John was friendly—a collaborator, passionately committed to teachers, students, learning, and culture building. John loved his job and was proud of the effective and dedicated professionals he worked with each day. He was considered to be a real up-and-comer in his district. One fall day, John received a call from his instructional supervisor, who wanted to discuss teacher walk-through observations. During the conversation, the central office staff member told John the division had hired a consultant who would come to John's school and several other schools to do walk-through observations of teachers.

"Our consultant will be at your school on Wednesday. Have a schedule created for him to visit as many classes as he can in fifteen-minute increments. I love this guy; he claims he can tell everything there is to know about a teacher's effectiveness in fifteen minutes. This will be so helpful! Also, and keep this to yourself, this consultant is a personal friend of the superintendent's."

John thought to himself, *How could anyone tell everything about a teacher in fifteen minutes?* "Who's going to accompany the consultant?" John asked. "And what do I tell teachers?" John had done a great job using walk-throughs in his building. Teachers worked in teams to develop improvement points they wanted to focus on, and at times, teachers would conduct walk-throughs to provide specific feedback on what their colleagues were trying to improve. Walk-throughs were helping teachers grow and build trust.

"We gotta surprise them, so don't tell them anything at all. You know, John, I expect big things from you in this division; I need your word that you will not tell your faculty about this." With reluctance and doubts, John agreed.

On Wednesday, John and the consultant visited classrooms in fifteen-minute increments all day except for lunch. Teachers were emailing John, asking, "Who is this guy?" Some sent John texts with similar messages. At 3:00 p.m., John was in a meeting, listening to how bad his teachers were. As John was driving home, he wondered how he could show his face in school the next day. All the work he had put into building trust and positive relationships was gone. Through no fault of his own, John found himself in a place where he had few options.

REFLECT ON TWO QUESTIONS

- How can John repair the break in trust with his faculty?
- What are the next steps John could take to help his supervisors know that walk-throughs and collaborative conversations have been successful in his school?

Trust and positive relationships within a school and with a central office are foundational to the success of a school and entire division, especially when you're asking for significant learning gains in literacy and numeracy. Without trust, failure increases (Covey & Merrill, 2006, p. 1). To build and enhance trust, you have to cultivate positive relationships. Effective principals demonstrate honesty, transparency, and integrity every day, believing in the old saying: *actions speak louder than words.* Remember that trusting relationships develop best when words are congruent with actions. Indeed, "the principal sets the tone for a school. The principal's behavior has a significant influence on the culture of the school" (Tschannen-Moran, 2004, p. 175). Trusting relationships should always be your priority. If an entire school division believes in the power of trusting relationships, then John could have shared with his faculty the conditions surrounding the consultant's walk-throughs and his honest assessment of the consultant's conclusions in order to rebuild trust among faculty.

Trusting relationships develop best when words are congruent with actions.

TRUSTING RELATIONSHIPS IMPROVE STUDENTS' MOTIVATION, ENGAGEMENT, AND LEARNING

Students who attend schools where they feel trusted and safe are more likely to view school positively but trust and positive relationships alone will not elevate learning (Howard et al., 2020; Robb & Robb, 2019). A faculty member who worked for me years ago connected very well with students; they all loved his class. The problem became evident after spending time in his classroom: students weren't learning. Yes, they were having fun; they liked their teacher, but games and telling jokes and stories frequently replaced reading and writing. Students' learning improves when there's a combination of trusting relationships and excellent teaching. Building trusting relationships and increasing teacher effectiveness are goals you can work on each day to elevate and maintain learning for all students.

Effective teachers impact learning (Allington & Johnston, 2002). Therefore, the more effective teachers you have in your school, the higher the students' performance. Effective teachers are better at helping students learn by meeting their diverse needs; they manage their classrooms well, students experience success and increased motivation to learn, and parents are happier. As your school's leader, your first step to improving instruction is to build trusting relationships among faculty and staff that can lead to teachers' motivation to develop more effective instruction and in turn improve students' learning. A teacher who feels appreciated, valued, empowered, respected, and cared for will take risks that result in trying research-tested practices that can positively affect all students' progress.

Imagine a three-legged stool. Remove one leg, and the stool wobbles; remove two legs, and it can't balance. When your focus is the three Cs—connecting, coaching, and communicating—you're building a three-legged stool that develops trusting relationships and a school community dedicated to supporting students and inspiring your faculty's desire to grow.

CONNECTING, COACHING, AND COMMUNICATING: PARTS OF A THREE-LEGGED STOOL

Explore the importance of connecting, coaching, and communicating with faculty, students, and parents to build a foundation of trusting relationships with and among the three groups. Strengthen these three legs—faculty, students, and parents—by continually supporting your entire school community and focusing members on students' learning and the social-emotional well-being of everyone.

FACULTY: THE STOOL'S FIRST LEG

A daily dedication to each one of the Cs can enhance trust, positive relationships, and improved communication, resulting in developing the conditions needed for effective teaching and students' desire to learn and improve.

CONNECTING

On each school day, there are meetings, issues raised by parents and teachers, and tasks that require your attention. With so much to do, having positive interactions with teachers might not be high on your "to do" list. However, opportunities for enhancing trust and positive relationships exist throughout your day even when you're in your office completing district forms, writing teacher evaluations, and responding to emails. Scan your daily schedule and make note of opportunities for short but positive in-person interactions and sending brief emails praising teachers for a contribution made during a meeting or an interaction with a student while you walked the halls or observed their class. Questions can also support this goal.

Excellent reminders for ensuring that you're connecting positively with faculty and staff and reflecting on questions can help you build trust and positive relationships. I've taped the questions that follow to my desk and frequently revisit them. Review these and add queries relevant to your leadership situation.

- *How are you connecting with your faculty virtually or during times when students and staff are at school?*

- *Are you making and modeling connections focused on teaching and learning?*

- *Are you visiting classrooms, observing instruction, and having conversations about instruction?*

- *Are you collaborating with teachers about research-based practices, data, and meeting students' needs?*

The connections you make with teachers and students transmit messages about what you value, and they offer opportunities to demonstrate your commitment to learning. Find ways every day to enhance trust and positive relationships with teachers, staff, and students.

COACHING

During my career, I have found that there is too much evaluation in education and not enough coaching. You won't elevate, support, and honor your faculty through once- or twice-a-year evaluations, but you can influence your faculty when you coach and provide timely feedback. The most useful feedback is specific. Providing information to teachers on students' active involvement soon after you visit a class can benefit instruction. Always start with positives you noticed and then set priorities, focusing on one element to improve. For example, I might say something like: *I noticed how attentive students were when you presented a think-aloud showing how you used context to determine the meaning of "serrated." Consider pairing up students and having them practice using context to figure out a different word's meaning.* As with much in education, it's all about how you present feedback to a teacher, and that's why I often ask myself: *What would a great coach do?*

Great coaches help their athletes improve; they often model moves, offer specific suggestions to improve performance, and pose questions shortly after the coaching session. Effective coaches care about their team, and like coaches, effective principals care about their faculty and school community. In addition to modeling, you can spark conversations linked to coaching by asking questions that provoke reflection—questions like the following:

- *When do you provide feedback about a coaching session?*

- *Why is it important that feedback related to coaching always open with positives you noticed?*

- *How does it help the teacher when you set priorities and ask them to reflect on one aspect of the lesson?*

- *When might you model your expectations?*

- *Should you partner the teacher with a colleague who can be a support and sounding board?*

Unlike formal evaluations, coaching is nonthreatening, for its purpose is to provide feedback that invites teachers to reflect and find possible solutions. The focus of most teachers is their students and helping each one do their best every time class meets. When the faculty knows how much you care through modeling trusting relationships, they'll be more receptive to coaching suggestions, questions, and reflecting on ways to move forward.

COMMUNICATING

As a principal, you have many formal communications with staff: meetings, emails, memos, video meetings, to name a few. They're all important, but don't underestimate the importance of one-on-one or small-group conversations that allow your faculty to know you and experience how much you value them and their suggestions. Each conversation you have with faculty lets them know you better and observe that all-important congruence between your words and actions. The following questions can encourage deeper thinking about your communication style:

- *Do you communicate information to faculty frequently?*

- *Why is it important for communications to be positive?*

- *How are you building trusting relationships through your communications?*

- *Are you setting priorities and asking teachers to improve on one aspect of an observed lesson?*

Be approachable, be a communicator, be a good listener, and build connections and relationships—these opportunities to connect through communication can open the door for more instructional conversations that can lead to learning gains for all students.

STUDENTS: THE STOOL'S SECOND LEG

Effective principals invest time getting to know the students and avoiding regressive punishments, such as the attendance model of threatening students with suspension or appearing in court if they don't attend school. The threat can at times force students to attend, but it can't compel them to invest in their learning. However, connecting, coaching, and communicating can develop students' desire to learn and be a productive part of your school community as they build trust and positive relationships with you, peers, teachers, and staff.

CONNECTING

Connections with students can occur throughout the day. Set aside a few days each week to greet students as they leave their school bus in the morning or as they board the school bus to head home in the afternoon. Have lunch with different classes or groups a few times a week, visit classes and interact with students, read aloud to classes, or attend sports events to cheer and support your school's teams. Include students in the morning announcements by inviting them to discuss a book they loved or announce an upcoming sports event or band concert. Reflect on these questions before starting your day—questions that foster connections with students:

- *Are you talking to different students each day when classes change?*

- *Do you invite student leaders to meet with you in your office and discuss issues?*

- *Have you considered serving breakfast or lunch for a few days to chat with students?*

- *Do you visit the library and interact with students?*

- *Are you visible enough during the day where students congregate?*

- *When you walk the halls of your school, do you say hello and acknowledge students you pass?*

COACHING

As the principal, you're coaching students for positive and negative reasons. Know that your interest in students can turn a negative, like low grades or not completing tasks, into positives. Often, students come to your office for behavior and academic infractions. By listening to their reasons and explanations and working through the issues with them, you're building trust though coaching and forging a lasting connection. You can meet with a group of students after school and shoot hoops or run the track—this is not coaching a sport, it's using the sport to coach for meaningful connections and turning around negative attitudes. Attend students' advisory and government meetings and provide feedback. To coach and make a difference, think about these questions:

- *How are you helping students invest in their learning?*
- *How are you connecting with students to build positive relationships?*
- *Are you sharing insights you've gained with students' teachers and their guidance counselor?*
- *Are you following up to ensure that students are acting on agreed suggestions?*

COMMUNICATING

Noticing and communicating all the positives you observe as you interact with students can lead to increased trust, positive relationships, and a desire to work hard in all classes. Noticing positive contributions of students can be to individuals, small groups, or an entire class and can include brief conversations or longer conversations in your office, emails, and in special circumstances, a written note. When you take the time to communicate the positives you noticed, you build trust and show students that you care about them and their learning. The questions that follow are reminders to communicate positives that impact students' learning and behavior:

- *Do you know students' names?*
- *Are you finding daily opportunities to communicate positives to students?*
- *Do you follow through when a teacher recommends you praise a student or the entire class?*
- *Do students initiate communications with you?*
- *Do you make time to meet with students when they request time with you?*
- *Are you an active listener who responds to what students say?*

Communication is a powerful way to connect with students, for they will come to know you by how you interact with them and their peers. As you set aside time and consider how you are connecting with students, think about the level of your connections with parents.

FAMILIES: THE STOOL'S THIRD LEG

Your interactions with families provide strong models for teachers and staff. Cultivating positive relationships with families asks you to include them in your school's life and communicate with them so they support their children's learning, teachers, and you.

An excellent way to foster the three Cs among your administrators and faculty is to discuss the benefits of home visits. Know that some teachers will be reluctant and wait to initiate home visits until they hear feedback from others.

After many collaborative conversations, teachers and administrators in my school decided to visit at least four homes during the year.

During an end-of-the-year faculty meeting, teachers and administrators debriefed their experiences with home visits. No staff member reported a bad experience. Connections occurred, trust developed, and many felt parents' views of teachers and administrators changed. As I think back on doing home visits, my faculty and I were doing the three Cs, but we didn't realize it. Faculty connected with families, communicated in their home instead of in school, and coached parents on ways to support their children, creating a connection not possible from a distance. My team was supporting the third leg of the stool, and the stool was standing! We had begun a new and for us innovative way to further connections with families that mattered and worked.

Your decisions and actions will open or close doors to families in your community. Effective communication to families has to be a team effort, and each teacher and staff member has a role in enhancing parent communications and connections.

LEADERSHIP TIP

Connections are important. The pandemic has created restrictions that may prohibit visiting a home. Consider a visit by administrators and teachers happening outside a house or apartment building to advance connections and communications with families.

RECONNECTING WITH PARENT SUPPORT NETWORKS

When schools return to a normal, daily schedule, your responsibility will be to restart parent committees and groups that weren't sustained during virtual and hybrid instruction. Committees meet sporadically during the school year to support a specific need such as breakfast for teacher appreciation day, whereas groups meet regularly. To bring these back, you can organize volunteers that include former members, new parents, teachers, school leaders, and you. The goal is for members to reflect on and discuss reorganizing committees and groups as well as create a schedule of meetings.

Parents, teachers, and staff frequently communicate with one another. Reserve time to collaborate with parent committees and groups and set specific guidelines for the frequency of newsletters, emails, notices posted on the school's website and calendar, and social media posts. In addition to frequency, discuss the benefits of having more than one set of eyes proofread a communication. Written information from parents to the school community is a reflection of you and your standards, and that's why it's important to have designated readers to review everything. By the time you read something, it should be almost or totally perfect.

COMMITTEES

Parent committees can further positive connections with you and your school because they give parents a voice. Invite them to meet and collaborate to generate committees your school needs, such as a communication committee to review the effectiveness of school–family communications or a library committee to run book fairs and process new books. You or another school leader should attend the meeting that discusses recommendations, so you know decisions that affect the school.

GROUPS

Many schools have not sustained formal parent groups during the pandemic. Consider how you can restart some traditional parent groups: advisory, athletics, band, drama, choir, field trips, parent-teacher organization, among others. You can use these questions to guide your school's work on bringing back parent committees and groups:

- *What types of committees and groups could be valuable post-pandemic and beyond?*

- *How will committees and groups communicate with you?*

- *Is there a structure for evaluating the work? Will you or another administrator be part of developing a meeting schedule?*

- *Where will meetings take place?*

- *How will committees and groups communicate with staff?*

- *How do you model your belief in connecting with families?*

When parents feel welcome and appreciated for their contributions to school life, you will find that they're delighted to join committees and groups and work on projects that benefit the entire school community.

COACHING FAMILIES

Every time you meet with a family about their child, you're coaching them by suggesting ways to deal with behavior, academic work, and attitudes toward school. When you discuss with families suggestions for summer enrichment programs or camps that tap into their child's interests, you're coaching. The programs organized by you and staff members that address families' questions on parenting, homework, and after-school sports and music programs, also coach parents. Reflect on these questions that relate to coaching to self-evaluate your role:

- *Do you have annual programs that target families and their needs?*

- *Have you met with faculty and other school leaders to discuss the importance of positive coaching when discussing students with families?*

- *Are there materials in your media center that would interest families?*

- *How does the librarian raise families' awareness of these materials?*

The concept of a school being a community of learners should also include families, and coaching is a way to extend families' knowledge of their children's learning and progress as well as your school's vision and mission.

COMMUNICATING WITH FAMILIES

Collaborate to review ways you and staff have communicated with parents during virtual and hybrid instruction and consider new ways to share information with families as schools return to a new normal. Consider newsletters, calendars, school and teacher websites, videos created by you, teachers, and the librarian, as well as social media. It's important for you to know about these communications to offer support, input, and feedback, and ensure that you monitor the frequency of each one. The quality and frequency of outreach communications are often an area for improvement, and the questions that follow can focus you on what's working and specific needs:

- *Does your school website match the excellence of your school?*

- *Can prospective home buyers and applicants for jobs learn about your school, its vision, mission, and staff by reviewing the website?*

- *How do you set guidelines for social media?*

- *Do you review the videos teachers and staff post on your website?*

- *Do you have guidelines for teachers' websites that meet the level of excellence of your school's website?*

- *Are school communications enhancing relationships with families or not?*

- *How can they be improved?*

- *How do you measure the level of satisfaction families have with communication?*

Communicating regularly with families can create a feeling among them that they are important and that you and your entire school community value their input and feedback.

LEADERSHIP TIP

Keep Families Front and Center

During the year, set aside time to have conversations with faculty and staff and revisit how they are connecting, coaching, and communicating with parents. Parent connections increase their support of your faculty and staff, curriculum, and initiatives, resulting in more engaged parents who value their child's teachers and learning.

CONNECTING, COACHING, AND COMMUNICATING: THREE POWERFUL TOOLS

The three Cs support establishing trusting relationships and can increase students' connections to their school and motivation to learn. How? When students develop a strong sense of community by developing trust and positive relationships with their teachers, administrators, and staff, their desire to be contributing members of their school's community increases. Engagement increases. Collaborating to learn, think critically, and problem-solve increases. The result can and should be learning gains for every student (Schaps, 2003).

Your belief in the value of strong communication, coaching, and connections can empower teachers and staff to create new ways to connect with families and provide information that keep the parents updated. When you're open to new ideas, you can see the need to adjust communication traditions—a lesson I learned from my school counselors.

SCHOOL COUNSELORS CHANGE PARENT COMMUNICATION

Each year school counselors would schedule several parent information sessions in the evening. Attendance was usually low despite advertising each one. Counselors' frustration increased, for preparing these events was time-consuming, and attendance continued to diminish. Our lead counselor asked if all counselors could record presentations on a computer, allowing parents to view their slides and hear discussion points. I applauded the idea.

Counselors posted their presentations on the counselor page of our school website, and parents could access and watch them at their convenience. Counselors and teachers used email to recommend specific presentations to parents. This was a game changer for our school—a new way to communicate that respected busy parents and met our goal of keeping them informed. Our counselors continued to host a few in-person parent events, but far fewer than in the past.

The best changes can come from staff and often motivate others to explore unique ways to keep parents informed— and that's exactly what happened. Grade-level teams recorded and shared with families informational meetings that included videos to watch and talk about with their children, an experiment to be conducted at home, upcoming units, tips for being interviewed by their child, and so forth. Teachers also reimagined our school newsletter and changed it from a traditional, text-heavy document with few images to a staff-designed newsletter created with

Google Slides. Today, our newsletter has images on both sides, less text, QR codes if parents want additional information, and links to videos and our school's social media accounts. Besides continuing to communicate important information to parents, school counselors turned their attention to supporting students' social-emotional needs during virtual and hybrid learning.

SOCIAL-EMOTIONAL NEEDS AND STUDENTS

Students' social-emotional needs are a priority of school counselors, but post-pandemic, they are more important than ever. As I write this chapter, more schools are transitioning slowly back to a new normal. The pandemic's length continues to impact the emotional well-being of students, teachers, staff, and families, and we'll continue to learn the emotional costs for years to come. You and your leadership team have a responsibility to work in partnership with students and their families to best meet the emotional needs of every child.

Frequently, during the pandemic, I would hear, "We need Maslow before Bloom," and these statements ring true. Students should feel safe in schools, and feeling safe includes caring for students' emotional needs. School counselors have a pivotal role in meeting the social and emotional learning (SEL) of your students, but counselors cannot work alone. The SEL needs of students will be better met if all staff nurture and help. Collaboration and coordination are essential as you and your leadership team study suggestions to support students.

Reflect on and discuss these questions and then collaborate to develop actions that support SEL in your school:

- Is your division using a specific program to meet SEL needs of the students, or is each school choosing its direction? Have programs been vetted for effectiveness?

- What does meeting student SEL needs look like in your school? How can you add to and/or improve what you're presently doing?

- How can you work with staff to understand students' needs and explain the collective effort required to support students? What indicators will you use to gauge whether the program is a success?

- How will you launch the school's program and communicate it to students and parents?

- How can you use teacher read-alouds to spark whole-class and small-group discussions of SEL?

The SEL needs of students will be better met if all staff nurture and help.

Challenging times can be opportunities to strengthen your team, increase understanding, and collaboratively work in new ways to support all the students. The best schools will have a plan based on the needs of the school and the community it serves. They will invest time in understanding the plan, providing professional development, and communicating the plan to build faculty and parent support. When students feel emotionally secure and socially accepted at school, their ability to concentrate on learning improves. Since teachers have a large role in students' SEL, you'll also want to attend to the well-being of faculty.

EMOTIONAL NEEDS OF YOUR FACULTY

Anxiety defined my staff when students who opted for hybrid learning returned to school. Teachers had concerns about students' safety and worried whether they would contract COVID-19 and infect family members at home. Concerns of teachers and staff grew, as did their stress and frustration levels. Safety standards became critical for students and staff, and my administrative team and I invested time working with our central office to establish safety protocols aligned with Centers for Disease Control and Prevention (CDC) recommendations. Again and again, I communicated our plans to faculty, staff, students, families, and the surrounding community. However, stress did not diminish, and I searched for ways to minimize it. Since a person cannot take care of others if they don't take care of themselves, encouraging teacher self-care became the focus of our school and many other schools across the country and globe.

Once again, my faculty stepped up to support each other by creating a staff wellness program. Frequent input by our school counselors and me encouraged staff to take time each day to work on their wellness and stress. Counselors developed a survey form for staff to log activities and then celebrate meeting goals. Physical education teachers also provided staff and students with fitness tips, healthy eating ideas, and suggestions for setting hydration goals. The model of sourcing our team was working. I didn't have all the ideas, but my team members did, and they felt empowered to share, lead, and use their expertise to strengthen every member of our school community. The best schools are like a family, and families take care of each other. The staff wellness program became an additional opportunity to connect, coach, communicate, build trust, and enhance relationships. When staff feel valued, cared for, and appreciated, they'll work harder for the school and elevate learning for all. My school's teachers, like teachers around the country, were heroes switching rapidly to remote learning and maintaining learning continuity.

You are responsible for supporting and caring for teachers, staff, students, and families affected by the pandemic. Remember that you are not the sole person meeting the emotional needs of your teachers, staff, students, and families. How you model meeting the needs of those in your care encourages them to do the same for all school community members.

At the start of the chapter, you read about John, a principal, who through no fault of his own, wound up in a place where he had to rebuild trust and positive relationships with many teachers in his school. Fortunately, John was able to rebuild connections with his staff because they know him and what he stands for. Staff in the school were quick to realize that the uncomfortable situation was not John's doing, and they had faith he would find a solution for their school.

After the uncomfortable debrief with the consultant, John took a chance and spoke with his superintendent. He explained the experience, how staff reacted, the awkwardness, and how the day caused challenges for the work he and his staff were doing and wanted to continue into the future. John assumed that since his superintendent liked the consultant, he would be met with a closed mind. Fortunately, John's superintendent believed in empowering principals, and in the importance of trust. The consultant didn't come back to John's school, and his team continued walkthrough visits in ways that were right for them, continuing to improve learning for all students. John learned an essential part of leadership: you have to be an advocate for your people, be candid and honest, and take risks. John and his faculty continue to elevate the schools' student-focused culture, and now the walk-through experience has turned into a valuable story for his teachers, a true story of how John acted as an advocate for them.

The more you model, through words and actions, your commitment to trust and building positive relationships, the harder it will be for others to break the bond you have with teachers, staff, students, and families. The principal sets the tone, models the culture, and communicates a shared story. This dedication to modeling what you believe influences others and ensures that the three-legged stool stands firmly in place to benefit students' learning gains through trust, positive relationships, and differentiated instruction with teachers and families.

HYBRID LEADERSHIP TIPS

By reaching out and nurturing relationships as well as empowering teachers, students, and staff, you can develop a school community that values trust and taking risks and places students at the center.

Relationship Building

- Consider using video meetings to discuss initiatives, challenges, and opportunities. Involve staff, even if you're separated. A school's culture can exist in a virtual and hybrid environment, but for this to happen, you must make it a priority and model what you want others to do.

- Form a student advisory group to connect with students and discuss a principal advisory group with teachers, asking each grade level to send you the names of several students who are leaders or have the potential to become leaders. Reach out to families of the selected students with a phone call and create a schedule to meet with the student group virtually twice each month.
- Discuss student connections with the staff. Learn what is successful and share ideas among your team to create better student–teacher connections and relationships during virtual and hybrid learning.

Parent Connections

- Organize a virtual parent communication committee.
- Review parent outreach from the school to homes.
- Use video to send some messages. Emails are great, but creating a mixture of communications will offer parents diverse ways of receiving information.

Social and Emotional Learning (SEL)

- Many students have been away from school for a long time. Don't wait until students return to launch a program. Work with your counselors and teachers to plan how to start reaching out to students and families to provide support. The example I shared about a staff program to support staff needs can exist virtually. Working with your staff to develop a virtual support program is an opportunity to collaborate, think creatively, and provide SEL for them.

CONSIDER THESE ACTIONS AND AIM HIGH

- Collaborate with a representative group from your faculty to review how your school is communicating with parents.

- Commit to modeling what you believe. List ways you can integrate modeling into your schedule.

- Invite parents to serve on a communication committee; set the stage by making clear that you want to learn, listen, and enhance connections.

- Create a list of five actionable ideas to enhance trust and relationships. How could each of the five lead to better conditions in your school to elevate learning?

- Examine available data with counselors to develop a program to meet the social-emotional needs of your students. Communicate the plan to teachers, staff, students, and families.

- Reflect on the consistency of your words and actions. Do you model what you believe?

- Review how you're implementing the three Cs and use the questions under each C to reflect and improve.

- Develop a list of strategies for promoting the well-being and the social-emotional strength of your faculty, students, and staff.

Closing Reminder

Trust and positive relationships between you, teachers, staff, and students form the foundation of developing strong connections, supportive coaching, and ongoing communications that reflect how much you value staying in touch with all members of your school community.

CHAPTER 4

Supporting Students and Staff Through Professional Learning

Like so many teachers new to the profession, I couldn't wait to start my first teaching job. My journey began as a middle school Civics teacher in Virginia. Civics was a favorite subject, and I assumed my students would feel the same way. I was naive. My first year of teaching challenged me, putting me in touch with my strengths and raising my awareness of weaknesses. Quickly and with clarity, I can recall memories of that first year, and one in particular stands out: my first student assessment. I taught my first Civics unit with pride—just as my high school teacher had taught me. Disappointment would be a good word to describe my feelings when most of my students failed the first test. I wasn't sure what to do. The next day I met with my administrator and told her how confused I felt and that perhaps this job wasn't for me. I recall explaining, "I taught the content well, but most students failed." My administrator quickly suggested I return the test to the students, allow them to correct it, and change their grade, 50–100 percent. If a student scored 60 on the test and corrected the test, their grade would be 80.

She leaned back on her chair and said, "Evan, I've seen this many times. Let them correct the test, then change their grade, and everyone will be happy."

When I reflect on my administrator's conversation and her suggestion, it's painfully clear that her advice was not great. My administrator meant well, but the solution she offered had nothing to do with students' learning or my role as a teacher to reflect and reteach. To be honest, reteaching wouldn't have meant much to me during my first year. I was comfortable with one way of teaching, and if students didn't get it, there was little I felt I could do.

My first year of teaching was devoid of professional learning, opportunities to explore effective teaching strategies, and how to engage and motivate students in their learning. The administrator's message to colleagues and me was to find ways for the students to pass; there was little discussion about my role in helping students learn. Not a story to be proud of, but it's mine. What I am proud of is that that year I started to read articles and books about teaching and learning and observed two Civics teachers in different districts. Professional learning quickly became my road map for improving instruction—and it still is today.

PROFESSIONAL LEARNING VERSUS PROFESSIONAL DEVELOPMENT

Professional learning is different from professional development. Professional learning deeply involves teachers reflecting on and improving their teaching so that every student can experience success. The keyword is "learning," often referred to as "staff development," implying that the facilitator's job is to "develop" the staff. This model's purpose is to transmit information about specific topics.

These presentations are often passive, delivered over a few hours, and frequently teachers don't receive follow-up.

Professional learning deeply involves teachers reflecting on and improving their teaching so that every student can experience success.

Professional learning is the opposite of staff development because the responsibility for learning rests with the teacher, not the facilitator. Professional learning implies that educators are professionals who continually enlarge their theory of how students learn and who keep up with research-based practices. Learning is ongoing and can be self-directed. However, the overarching purpose of professional learning is to impact teacher efficacy and students' progress. Also, professional learning can affect collective efficacy in a school and division and result in further learning gains for students. In John Hattie's Visible Learning® research, collective teacher efficacy is a formidable force. Hattie ranked 150 influences related to students' learning outcomes and determined the average effect size was 0.40. However, the effect size of collective efficacy was 1.39. When teachers believe they can positively affect students and create environments valuing relationships, collaboration, creativity, and professional learning, students' learning improves.

THE IMPORTANCE OF PROFESSIONAL LEARNING

Professional learning enhances the skills of educators and is the foundation of an effective school and division. When teachers improve their skill, they bring to their students more strategies for assisting, guiding, and supporting learning. Quality professional learning can increase teachers' belief in the capacity of their students, boosting teachers' confidence in increasing learning gains for all the students. You have a role and responsibility to elevate the efficacy your teachers have and one way to accomplish this goal is through quality professional learning. By failing to promote teacher efficacy, you run the risk of perpetuating this self-fulfilling prophecy: teachers who don't believe they can improve the lives of students don't succeed at reaching this goal (Ashton & Webb, 1986; Eells, 2011).

During the pandemic, some schools across America stopped professional learning entirely or shifted the focus toward the professional technology development needed to triage a quick shift to remote learning. Many schools moved away from long-range goals, focusing on how to make it day by day. The changes in the spring of 2020, more than any time in recent history, altered the way educators did their job. These changes also heightened glaring disparities: students with access to the Internet and a device to attend virtual classes and those with no device or Internet access. The rapid change created many challenges for teachers, such as managing virtual and/or hybrid instruction, lack of student success, safety concerns, emotional needs, keeping students engaged, attendance, and reliability of the technology they used. Unusual times can call for quick decisions, and one of these, in some divisions, was to diminish the role of professional learning.

This chapter offers a pathway to bring professional learning back to your school or to enhance what is currently in place. The model of professional learning is collaborative and can improve teaching in your school. Success starts with your leadership.

THE PRINCIPAL'S ROLE MATTERS

Consider how you can start professional learning collaboratively and maintain this focus throughout the year. Climate, culture, trust, and relationships are factors positively influencing or inhibiting professional learning in your school. They are factors you control. What follow are three personal and professional standards for you to embrace because they shine a spotlight on professional learning and how it influences students' engagement. Be the intentional leader who understands that your support of ongoing professional learning improves instruction.

1. Make ongoing professional learning essential.
2. Participate and become a learner among learners.
3. Empower staff to take a leadership role to further professional learning in your school.

When you collaborate with teachers to develop professional learning opportunities, you'll identify choices that meet the needs of all teachers. Start slowly and carefully gauge teachers' reactions to ensure they feel they have choices that support their needs.

A MENU OF PROFESSIONAL LEARNING

Developing a range of professional learning techniques based on teachers' input ensures that everyone, from new to seasoned teachers, can find a professional learning experience that benefits them. Moreover, a menu of choices permits teachers to move forward with their professional learning at a pace that works for their time frames. What you're doing is differentiating teachers' learning and at the same time honoring their voices and choices.

Consider two pathways for professional learning. The first can be based on school initiatives created with your teachers. Or, you can survey teachers and have conversations with them to understand specific areas unique to their content, team, or department. Your goal should be to focus on improving teaching and student learning through choice. Choice empowers teachers to learn in a manner best for them and consistent with the choice teachers offer students. When you and teachers understand the reasons for professional learning, you can develop a menu using the ten ways to foster and build professional learning experiences. On page 79, you'll find a resource box listing materials popular with teachers in my school.

SCHEDULING PROFESSIONAL LEARNING

The benefits of providing a menu of choices permits teachers to decide the best time to collaborate and learn: during a department or team meeting, before or after school. They can read and interact with the group on Google Docs or read diverse materials and then have groups discuss these at full faculty meetings.

BOOK STUDY

A book study can be the same book for all teachers or three to four different books that differentiate professional learning. You can select a book that you believe will speak to all teachers, or you can ask teams and/or departments to select one to two books and invite teachers to choose a book and group they'd like to join.

Consider your role in a book study—be a participant and let one teacher or a rotation of teachers lead discussions. The best book studies allow teachers to move through the book in sections followed by conversations. Having members reflect on the following question can lead to their trying a new practice or refining one they're using: *How can I integrate this information into my teaching to improve students' learning?*

ARTICLE STUDY

If your school has limited funds for professional learning, articles are an excellent choice, for there are many available on the Internet that can be accessed by putting a topic into a search engine. Like book studies, an article study can be the same article or three to five related articles on aspects of a topic such as critical thinking or a schoolwide initiative on solving math word problems. To generate excitement and enthusiasm for article studies, I recommend starting them at school. I have found that teachers often continue to explore articles on their own or with a group of colleagues. For example, our school initiative was grading, and I shared with teachers several articles and reflection questions, asking them to choose three to read and invited groups to discuss them at the faculty meetings. Teachers enjoyed discussing different articles in their groups and considering diverse perspectives on grading.

BLOGS

By searching the Internet, teachers can quickly generate a robust list of educational blogs about topics related to your school initiative or topics of interest to them. Include blogs you follow on the master list. Encourage teachers to share a favorite blog on a Google Doc with everyone or a specific group. At each faculty meeting, ask teachers and staff to share a blog post or a new blog they have discovered. Blogs remain a great way to learn ideas and opinions from other educators and connect you and your staff to educators across the nation and world. My blog started with my mother, Laura Robb, when we decided to share our reading and writing ideas from the principal's and literacy coach's perspectives. Reading blogs can inspire one or a few teachers in your school to create one!

INSTRUCTIONAL VIDEOS

When a school has a culture of professional learning, teachers often want to explore new instructional strategies and techniques that can improve their practice and students' learning. Raise teachers' awareness of the many instructional videos available on the Internet for them to observe and discuss with colleagues by recommending videos about the Socratic method, effective questioning techniques, KWL (What do I know? What do I want to know? What have I learned?) strategies, project-based learning, and much more. Also, teachers can take a video of themselves teaching a strategy or technique and share it with colleagues in your school or with a much larger audience by posting their lesson on YouTube.

TED TALKS

Challenge staff to think differently about many issues impacting people, education, and our world by sharing and discussing TED and TEDx videos. TED allows you and your team to learn from some of the world's most creative thinkers for no cost at all. Have faculty and staff watch a video during a scheduled meeting as a springboard to discussing unique ways of thinking about teaching and learning. You can also recommend specific TED videos by emailing teachers or through conversations during meetings and conferences. As you share, you'll observe teachers and staff suggesting to each other TED videos they have found. Eventually, many will organize team and/or department viewings to discuss new ways of thinking that can support students' growth.

PODCASTS

A few years ago on my twenty-minute drive to and from work, I started listening to podcasts. Podcasts soon became a professional learning opportunity for me each day, enriching my daily commute. Listening to and learning from educators about successes and challenges was motivating, providing me with ideas for reflection. One fall morning, in a casual discussion, I realized that a teacher in my school was a fan of a podcast I had not heard. I told him I'd listen, and to reciprocate, I shared a favorite podcast with him. This led to short conversations about the podcasts between the teacher and me, and soon we were sharing our favorites at team, department, and full faculty meetings. Create a shared folder for staff to add podcasts they enjoy, which would result in multiple opportunities and choices for teachers to listen, discuss, learn, and reflect!

WEBINARS

The pandemic has elevated the use of webinars to share ideas on teaching, learning, and leading. Many well-known educators have free live webinars or recorded webinars available for anyone to access. Social media is an excellent way to find webinars on many educational topics. Each month I have a goal of sourcing two webinars and sharing them with teachers. I don't require webinar attendance, but I do encourage that they take advantage of this free professional learning! My role is to find the opportunities, share, and communicate how the topic relates to school initiatives or goals specific to a content area. You will find that staff will be more likely to learn from webinars when you assist with finding opportunities for them and explaining the webinar's relevance.

IDEA EXCHANGES

These work best if you initiate them after a few months of school. Ask a teacher leader to create a shared folder and invite faculty from across the curriculum to consider writing up one to two successful lessons. Teachers learn from one another and always have the option to reach out to a colleague to ask questions about a specific lesson. Besides lessons, the exchange can highlight favorite read-aloud texts, poems, short videos, websites, short stories, and articles. Such schoolwide sharing offers multiple opportunities for teachers to learn from and support one another with the goal of increasing students' learning gains.

SOCIAL MEDIA

Professional learning networks such as Twitter, Facebook, and Instagram offer school leaders, teachers, and staff multiple opportunities to learn from educators around the world—and the connections and learning can occur from any smartphone. Remember, when your faculty and staff are active on social media, they represent your school and the district, so it's important to have ongoing discussions to develop policies for what's appropriate to post, including content and photos of students and colleagues. These aren't one-and-done conversations but should be revisited a few times during each school year to discuss new platforms and revisit policies for platforms already in use. Social media can expand connections to school leaders and educators and bring dozens of unique voices to professional learning in your school. You can encourage teachers to use social media to create and increase connections, learn, and share ideas through modeling and by meeting with small groups for an in-person idea exchange.

PROFESSIONAL CONFERENCES

Sending teachers to a conference can enhance their instructional practices and motivate them to grow, and the dollars spent can become cost-effective when the teachers share, in depth, their experiences with other faculty. The pandemic has caused in-person conferences to shift to Web-based events. As we move out of the pandemic, traditional conferences may be redefined to meet educators' needs. Like you and many principals, I have a tight budget, and though valuable, conferences can be expensive. Be targeted with your limited funding and seek conferences to meet the literacy and numeracy needs agreed upon by you and your teachers.

However, if there's an Edcamp near your school, try one out. Edcamps are free and create nontraditional ways for educators to learn and share information. If your faculty is new to the idea of Edcamps, share a video easily found on the Web and attend an Edcamp with teachers interested in a nonconventional professional learning experience. When I attended an Edcamp with some of my teachers, their enthusiasm for the experience caused them to team up with our tech staff and me to develop an Edcamp for educators in our division and surrounding areas.

A menu of professional learning experiences offers choices and the option to start at teachers' comfort level and move forward. In the following box, you'll find professional materials to explore and share with faculty. However, consider creating a shared folder available to faculty and staff and invite them to add materials to this starter list.

PROFESSIONAL BOOKS, VIDEOS, AND TEDTALKS TO EXPLORE

Below are several my teachers and I have learned from and enjoyed, but equally important, have impacted students' learning gains.

PROFESSIONAL BOOKS

- *Mindset: The New Psychology of Success* by Carol S. Dweck
- *180 Days: Two Teachers and the Quest to Engage and Empower Adolescents* by Kelly Gallagher and Penny Kittle
- *The Quick Guide to Simultaneous, Hybrid, and Blended Learning* by Douglas Fisher, Nancy Frey, John T. Almarode, and Aleigha Henderson-Rosser

VIDEOS

- TeacherTube
- Sourced videos from YouTube

TEDTALKS

- TEDEd on YouTube is an excellent hub of thought-provoking talks on education
- A favorite TEDx talk: "How Great Leaders Inspire Action" by Simon Sinek

LEADING THE CHANGE FOR PROFESSIONAL LEARNING

The ten ideas listed for professional learning provide options for you to model as you learn with your teachers—options from books and Internet resources to costly conferences. The professional learning journey you embark on with your teachers can transform your school into an ever-evolving learning center. You and your teachers can inspire and empower one another to learn, collaborate, communicate, analyze data, and think critically. Armed with this skill set, you better prepare your students to be reflective and become critical thinkers as well as lifelong learners who can become the creative problem solvers our world will need.

For a professional learning program to flourish and reach the needs of teachers in your school, you must support the concept and commit to participating in learning experiences with them. The following leadership traits can enable you to develop and nurture a professional learning community:

- Listening to teachers and responding to their needs.
- Empowering the faculty to organize and lead school-based, professional learning.
- Involving the teachers in the decision-making process for professional learning.
- Believing that improved instruction can benefit all students.
- Understanding that change takes time.
- Building commitment instead of demanding compliance.

- Valuing trust by creating a safe environment for teachers and staff to change.

- Encouraging and modeling risk taking.

- Finding budget money to support professional learning.

By becoming a learner among learners, you reveal how much you value professional learning as a pathway to improving instruction and students' progress.

If moving to student-centered learning is a goal most faculty embrace, you'll want them to experience collaborative discussions of materials that increase their knowledge of research-tested instructional practices for literacy and numeracy. When teachers experience what students will do, they gain invaluable insights into the process.

ELEVATE PROFESSIONAL LEARNING: REDEFINE FACULTY MEETINGS

Thinking differently can lead to new and better learning opportunities for teachers, improving learning for students. Faculty meetings present an opportunity for change. Consider your faculty meetings or faculty meetings you recall from the past. I recall meetings where the principal stood in front of his teachers with a yellow legal pad and relayed information and any item he felt necessary to share. These were meetings with no interaction, collaboration, or professional dialogue.

Today, when email can connect teachers and staff with ease, much of the administrative information shared in traditional faculty meetings can be communicated in an email, presenting an innovative opportunity to rethink the focus of full faculty meetings. Consider how your faculty meetings can enhance your school's professional learning goals by generating ways to support instruction, students' social emotional well-being, and their academic progress.

PROFESSIONAL LEARNING FACULTY MEETINGS

Meetings are the ideal place for teachers to experience learning the way you hope students will learn in their classrooms. As teachers experience collaboration, notebook writing, analytical and creative thinking, and choice, they gain the skill needed to effectively implement a student-centered approach and at the same time impact students' learning.

To help you begin the change process, I suggest that you set aside time for four faculty meetings for teachers to experience student-centered learning and connect what they've learned in classroom practices. During these meetings, you, your administrative team, and teachers will collaborate with each other, choose materials, think critically, and transfer their learning to adjust and refine their instructional practices.

Before the first meeting, select topics of study either aligned with school initiatives or drawn from discussions with staff members. To start with, find an article that connects to your goals for each topic. Have chart paper or a large whiteboard available for groups to document their discussions. Review the first four meeting tips for ideas on transforming principal-controlled meetings into professional learning faculty meetings.

MEETING 1

- Organize faculty and school leaders into four groups of four to six, and introduce the available topics. Offer each group a choice of topic and provide the article related to their topic. Groups then read and discuss the article.

- Each group selects a spokesperson to share with the other groups what their group discussed. Invite a volunteer to record ideas on chart paper or a whiteboard.

- Ask and challenge groups to discuss ways they could create or incorporate the topic from the article into classroom instruction and how the new ideas could improve student learning. The goal is to bring intentional change to the classroom. The first meeting can end with a goal that each group will share at the next meeting: how the new strategy or practice worked in their classes, including successes and challenges.

MEETING 2

- Review the reasons for why the content and organization of meetings have changed and how energized you are to have professional discussions with the faculty.

- Review recorded ideas on chart paper from the first meeting to recap discussions.

- Invite teachers to share a lesson to demonstrate how they incorporated a new strategy or practice learned in the first meeting. Invite questions.

- Ask groups to read and discuss a new article focused on initiatives or school needs you and your staff want to further explore. Encourage staff to consider how they could use these ideas in their classrooms.

- Groups choose a new spokesperson who shares discussion points with the larger group. Ideas are recorded on a chart paper or a whiteboard.

- For the remainder of the meeting groups, including you and other administrators, discuss how to integrate these ideas into classrooms and challenge participants to try something learned from the article study before the next faculty meeting.

MEETING 3

- Recap and bring back to focus what the group discussed at the second meeting by reviewing what was discussed and posted by each group.
- Invite teachers to share ideas from the first and second meetings that they used in their classrooms. What went well? What were some challenges?
- Choice has been part of the professional learning faculty meeting meetings. Ask groups to discuss how they integrate choice into their curriculum and the daily learning opportunities for students.

MEETING 4

- Each meeting is a recap opportunity. A clear recap keeps everyone on the same page and allows you to communicate the story of change.
- Ask teachers to reflect on their experiences, discussions, and articles read, and create a list of

instructional practices and strategies they'll add to lessons in their classrooms.

- Ask groups to share ideas with the larger group, calling on a volunteer to record ideas. Encourage teachers to add ideas to their list if they hear an interesting idea from another group that might work in their classroom.

My examples of professional learning faculty meetings aren't completely invitational. Teachers and administrators can choose a topic that defines their group, but each meeting challenges them to try a new practice or strategy presented in their article. Teachers leave the meeting knowing that during the next meeting, they will be sharing lessons with their group and the entire faculty. As you think about change and restructuring faculty meetings, reflect on these additional questions:

- Are your actions creating an environment in which you encourage change?

- Are you communicating why there's a need for change without upsetting those who are happy with how things are?

- In what ways are you celebrating teachers who positively embrace change?

Learning is an ongoing process. Learning together through redefined faculty meetings is one more way to build a more robust learning-focused team. The repetition of learning together can change your school culture, defining the commitment of you and your staff to learning, practicing, sharing, and doing everything it takes to meet every student's needs.

ACCEPT WHERE TEACHERS ARE

Ask yourself: *How would this model change the dynamic for my faculty meetings?* Change can be big or small, but if you do nothing to initiate change, don't expect a different result.

At the core of this chapter is how you can be a catalyst for positive change and boost learning by improving and enhancing teachers' instructional skill. Even though new possibilities may make you and your faculty enthusiastic, it's important to remember that change is a process, not an event. Process takes time, and some will be more willing than others to consider change.

Equally important, reflect deeply on how you plan to bring staff together when division exists. When you start an article study for a faculty meeting or a book study with a group of teachers, consider what strategies you might use to bring each person and group along. You might meet with small groups to hear their perspectives on change, offer them articles to read, and then meet with them to discuss the articles and encourage them to be open to learning and change. Even after reading and discussing the articles, some may not be ready to change. Background knowledge, level of investment, and personal experiences will determine their understanding. Be positive. Make sure you notice small changes in attitudes and offer positive feedback in emails or through conversations. Ultimately, helping staff grow professionally is founded on the same foundational elements needed to be successful as a leader.

Relationship building: When the positive connections you make with teachers are ongoing, you develop trusting relationships with them and can lobby for changes. Human connections are foundational for successful classrooms and schools.

Modeling your beliefs: Each day, modeling for teachers what you believe through words and actions communicates to teachers what you value. If you model an interest in learning, growing, and a willingness to change, teachers will feel comfortable trying new practices and strategies.

Change can be daunting. Your willingness to change can help teachers rethink their present instructional practices and experience something new. Today's students live in a world of rapid changes. The skills students need to solve local, national, and world problems will be met by leaders like you who inspire teachers to commit to enhancing their instructional skill set to increase the learning gains of all students.

HYBRID LEADERSHIP TIPS

Professional Learning

Hybrid or virtual schools should continue professional learning opportunities for the faculty. The initiatives created collaboratively by you and teachers can be adjusted and developed through video platforms and allowing conversation about shared documents. Because professional learning is more successful when it's relevant to teachers' needs, during the pandemic many schools shifted professional learning to an increased focus on the technology needed for virtual learning. Be flexible as you work with the teachers to provide additional relevant experiences.

(Continued)

Some schools have let go of professional learning during the pandemic. I don't recommend dropping coordinated learning for teachers to meet all students' needs, but you should recognize the need for fewer focus areas to lighten the load for teachers. Virtual and hybrid teaching is hard work; teachers are taxed and tired. Discover teachers' needs, start small, and use the technology available to you to create opportunities to collaborate, share, and grow.

Professional Learning Faculty Meetings

During the pandemic, most schools shifted faculty meetings to virtual meetings. You'll use virtual faculty meetings to share information that you might not need to share post-pandemic such as mask protocols, schedules changing mid-year, ventilation questions, and strangers accessing synchronous teacher meetings. No doubt, faculty meetings during the pandemic are different. However, you can still share information for staff to reflect on and learn. Once a month, during a virtual faculty meeting, consider inviting teachers to read and discuss an article at the meeting and explain why you believe it supports teaching and student learning. Or you can invite teachers to read the article at their convenience and let them know that at the next meeting they can discuss and share their thoughts about the article and how it might impact their instruction.

CONSIDER THESE ACTIONS AND AIM HIGH

- Collaborate with a representative group from your faculty and create professional learning goals for your school and teacher groups.

- Commit to being an active participant in all of the school's professional learning.

- Invite teachers to share ideas during professional learning faculty meetings.

- Create a list of five professional learning opportunities from my list of ten choices—opportunities that meet your school's needs.

- Examine roadblocks to change. Generate ideas with faculty to help you overcome them.

- Reflect on professional learning in your school, identify the most pressing issue facing your school, and collaborate to explore possible learning experiences.

- Examine your leadership to assess how your school's culture encourages teachers to participate in professional learning. Develop a list of positives and needs and set two priorities to work on now.

- Develop a team of teachers to find articles on topics faculty has expressed a desire to study. Use these articles to change the focus of faculty meetings to collaborative learning.

Closing Reminder

As the principal, you'll always have several priorities to juggle and address. However, keeping professional learning that develops from teachers' needs and suggestions is an effective way to increase teachers' instructional skill set and meet the diverse needs of your student population.

CHAPTER 5

Creating a Culture of Access, Equity, and High Expectations

The library in your school should be its family room—a place where students, teachers, staff, and parents can gather to read, converse, interact, research, and enjoy the company of others. Such a library is different from those in my school experience. From elementary through high school, most libraries from my past were quiet spaces where students checked out and returned books, had a silent study hall, or featured a monthly class on the Dewey Decimal System and research techniques. Today, to meet the needs of all students, libraries serve diverse purposes: they are media centers and have makerspaces for creative and critical thinking and self-directed learning. In addition, there are areas for collaboration, shelves of books, book displays to engage students, a green screen for playing videos of book talks, and of course, sofas and chairs and pillows where students read.

Post-pandemic school libraries will most likely have guidelines to limit how many students can be in that space at the same time. However, the library can still serve as the family room of your school. It'll be different, but with imagination, the space can enrich the reading lives of students and teachers.

The collaborative relationships among the librarian, administrators, and teachers are key to effectively utilizing the space to create opportunities to learn, for cultural diversity, access, and equity, and to support the high expectations you and your staff have for students. Collaboration with your librarian can help your school achieve goals, even during challenging times.

Recently, I discussed the need to review school and classroom library collections for cultural diversity with our school librarian, Alysia Deem. "Reading will be an enhanced focus for our school when more students return; this is good time to review all collections of books."

Alysia nodded. "I've already started reviewing book collections with an emphasis on our school goal of bringing more diversity to them. I'll have a proposal for us to review in a week; it'll include strengths of our collections and where we need additional books."

"That's great; let's continue our practice of finding books with a wide range of readability. I know this may be costly, but I'll do my best to find funds to support this."

We reserved a day on the following week to review the proposal. The cost was high. However, we prioritized the request to purchase books based on the highest needs. Later that day, I called Alysia. "Let me know your thoughts on how to raise teacher awareness of the new books added to collections and your ideas on how I can provide support."

"Thanks, Evan. We have a virtual faculty meeting on Monday. I can share information at this meeting, and you and I can have a separate meeting with ELA teachers to share how some of the books fit with their genre-based unit plans."

"Sounds great. At the faculty meeting, I'll speak first about the reading initiative, our school commitment to increase cultural diversity, and I'll share some points from Richard Allington on volume in reading and choice. Then I'll turn it over to you."

The initial meetings with faculty and ELA teachers started conversations with them about classroom libraries, new additions to the central library, the importance of reading in all subjects, and bringing culturally diverse reading opportunities to students. Books that students can read and books that raise cultural awareness contribute to developing empathy and a reading identity.

ACCESS, EQUITY, HIGH EXPECTATIONS, AND TRUSTING RELATIONSHIPS

The word "all" is simple, but it can spur significant change. My conversation with Alysia offers insights into a leadership style embedded in this book: a commitment to collaboration, partnerships, communication, and a desire to provide access and equity for the reading and learning experiences of all students. When a school collectively commits to providing access to books for all students, mindsets can shift and expectations change.

Perhaps, you had some school experiences similar to mine. Everyone read the same text, listened to the same lesson, and did the same assignments—quizzes and tests focused on memorizing information. This was evident in English classes where all students read the same book, even if everyone couldn't read it, and a fear of failure became the motivator. Research on differentiation (Robb, 2016; Tomlinson, 2017) and student-centered classrooms (Miller, 2020) has changed instruction, yet instructional practices that don't support all students remain.

Change requires belief, optimism, and high expectations. But first, you need to gain an understanding of what high expectations are for yourself and your school, as well as what they aren't. High expectations for test scores can be limiting; high expectations for attendance are important but could be considered narrow. Conversely, high expectations for access and equity, collaboration, critical and analytical thinking, problem solving, creativity, and engagement show the complexity of this concept. High expectations can raise the bar, but you must know what the bar is. Esther Quintero noted, "If we are serious about raising expectations for all learners, we need to think seriously about what expectations are, how they work, and what it might take to create environments that *equalize* high expectations for what students can achieve" (Quintero, 2014). High expectations can easily be added to the list of overused terms that are hard to define and still harder to actualize. But if you collectively define what high expectations mean for your school, the impact can be profound. Consider how your words and actions can help your school maintain a focus on high expectations when students' learning is the school's core goal. Lambert portrays the principal as the fire carrier for the school's vision and a leader who models the school's expectations and desire for collaboration (2000). A fire carrier of a school's vision and belief in learning for all are the foundation that elevates equity and access.

Leaders who model agreed-upon high expectations for their schools' focus use three characteristics identified by

Blasé and Kirby (2000): (1) optimism, (2) honesty, and (3) consideration. All three are critical to building personal relationships conducive to effective reform efforts, such as collectively creating high expectations.

OPTIMISM

A belief in a better future can have a substantial impact on your school. Many leaders have learned that it can be hard or appear disingenuous if one tries to be too positive during challenging times, but all leaders can be optimistic about the future.

HONESTY

Leaders who are truthful and have consistency between words and action can enhance trusting relationships with teachers, staff, and students. Your honesty won't always make everyone happy, but remember that conversations are a great way to increase understanding and acceptance. Successful leaders speak the truth.

CONSIDERATION

Considerate leaders are empathetic listeners and demonstrate care and concern for those on their team. Teacher leaders demonstrate the same characteristics when working with children.

A focus on optimism, honesty, and consideration provides a framework for empowerment. Within the framework, you communicate expectations, coach, converse, listen, empathize, and support faculty and students. This creates a heightened understanding and buy-in of the school's expectations, allowing you to empower teacher leaders to amplify your school's message of access and equity to colleagues, students, and families.

BOOKS CREATE ACCESS AND EQUITY

Schools that have 1:1 technology initiatives, well-trained staff, computers, and handheld devices available remain distinctly advantaged over rural and impoverished parts of the country where access to broadband and computers for students may be limited. Since virtual learning won't occur for students who don't have access to a computer and the Internet, it presents a unique leadership challenge for you, your teachers, and educators worldwide. Unfortunately, inequity is not new in education, and zip code often diminishes educational opportunities in public schools and the workplace. As Jonathon Kozol explains: "I wanted to make clear that if there is something savage in America, it is in the powerful people who are willing to tolerate these injustices" (1992, p. 4). With optimism and some degree of hope, the pandemic may spur additional conversations about funding and opening doors to increase access and equity for students no matter where they live.

While we wait for change, there is work to do. Course opportunities, materials, technology, and professional learning are factors influencing access and equity in school—factors you, teachers, and staff can control. The best schools don't blame external factors such as home life, parent support, or last year's teachers to explain poor student performance. Instead, they focus on what they can do to create opportunities for students, as noted by Hoy et al. (2002): "Collective efficacy was more important in explaining school achievement than socio-economic status." This research gives hope and supports the positive impact of committed professionals who believe they can make a difference. Still, it doesn't justify the financial imbalances that exist in American schools—imbalances that cause a lack of books, materials, professional learning opportunities, and skilled teachers.

One way to create better opportunities for students is to review the books and the role of books in ELA classrooms and beyond in your schools as noted by Dr. Rudine Sims Bishop:

> Books are sometimes windows, offering views of worlds that may be real or imagined, familiar or strange. These windows are also sliding glass doors, and readers have only to walk through in imagination to become part of whatever world has been created and recreated by the author. When lighting conditions are just right, however, a window can also be a mirror. Literature transforms human experience and reflects it back to us, and in that reflection, we can see our own lives and experiences as part of the larger human experience. Reading, then, becomes a means of self-affirmation, and readers often seek their mirrors in books. (1990, pp. ix–xi)

Meeting students' reading needs offers them opportunities to learn, understand, and see themselves in texts. Reading also enables students to step into the skin of characters and people from other cultures and lifestyles and develop understanding and empathy for them. Once students have access to culturally diverse materials they can learn from, you move a step closer to equity and access and can start actualizing the high expectations teachers have for students. Teachers should understand the role of books in your school, and it's important to examine books to ensure they represent all the cultures and lifestyles in our country.

EXAMINING MATERIALS
FOR ACCESS AND EQUITY

Students deserve equal access to learning materials and skilled teachers no matter where they live or what school they attend. Your challenge is balancing and prioritizing access and equity in a job where on any given day events and issues can make it difficult to focus on important initiatives. However, if you don't consider and continually act on the more significant challenges that affect all students, change won't occur. Beware of this pitfall: Changes such as access and equity can be put on hold and continue because they've always been in place or under the veil of tradition. Avoid the pitfall by sharing the leadership and asking the library staff and ELA teachers to review the school's book collections through a lens of cultural diversity, access, and equity. To help you create a diverse book collection for independent and instructional reading and daily read-alouds, reflect on these seven questions (Robb, 2022):

1. Do books include main and minor lesbian, gay, bisexual, transgender, queer, and intersex characters, disabled characters, characters of color, and characters representing the cultural diversity in our country and the world?

2. Are the books historically and culturally accurate?

3. Do the books' authors and illustrators represent diverse cultures and lifestyles?

4. Does your collection include picture books, poetry, fiction, nonfiction, essays, and drama?

5. Do the books serve as "mirrors, windows, and sliding glass doors" for all students in your classes? (Sims Bishop, 1990)

6. Will the book lead students to depth of thinking and hold the possibilities of changing their beliefs or increasing their empathy and understanding?

7. Do books already in your collections contain racial, ethnic, and societal stereotypes in the text and/or images? How do you plan to counter these stereotypes?

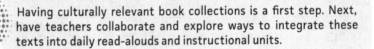

Having culturally relevant book collections is a first step. Next, have teachers collaborate and explore ways to integrate these texts into daily read-alouds and instructional units.

Questions guide conversations and can lead adult and student learners to reflect, adjust, and affirm, and then pose more questions. The questions for review of books and book collections can guide ELA and content area teachers as they discuss curriculum, materials, access, diversity, and equity. As you and your teachers evaluate curriculum and content, consider the questions in the ACCESS acronym that follows and use them as a guide to collaborative decision-making.

- **Appropriate levels for students:** How will you determine whether the materials meet the reading needs of students? Can materials be differentiated to meet a range of reading abilities?

- **Connections to curriculum and cultures:** How are teachers creating curricular connections to other cultures and lifestyles? Are students receiving equal exposure and experiences, or is what they learn dependent on who teaches them?

- **Content accuracy:** When considering supplementary materials, what process does the school have to review information for accuracy, stereotyping, and bias?

- **Effective costs:** Budgets have limits—how do you prioritize yours? Are you collaborating and gathering feedback to assist your decisions and support the needs of teachers?

- **Subjects with different viewpoints:** How is your school teaching critical and analytical thinking and providing students with the tools to make thoughtful decisions? Are teachers helping students identify fake news and propaganda? Are students becoming discerning consumers of information?

- **Special needs students and English language learners:** Does your school have materials that are accessible to all students no matter their ability level or disability? Are access and equity for all a key part of your school's mission and vision?

During my first year as a principal, I encountered these barriers to what I'm proposing you consider:

- English teachers taught the same three to four books each year because they liked them and had completed all the lesson plans.

- History teachers lectured from frayed legal pads filled with notes that had been developed years ago.

- The school's library had a small collection of books, and only a few represented the cultural diversity in our country.

- Parents admired teachers for their strict, unbending rules and instructional practices, but students feared and distrusted them.

There were times when these barriers seemed insurmountable, but you can cope with and change them by finding a place to start. Much of leadership begins with a step, a question, a conversation. Consider how to motivate teachers and create the professional engagement and buy-in that can result from asking, reflecting on, and discussing difficult questions that can slowly lead to significant changes.

Teachers' motivation to change can kick-start commitment that can lead to learning and then rethinking and reevaluating their practices and beliefs. Motivated and engaged teachers collaborate with colleagues and school leaders to develop theories of how students learn—theories based on research. When their commitment to change is intentional, their motivation and engagement drive the moves they take to transfer what they've learned into instructional practices that support all students.

SEVEN PILLARS OF ENGAGEMENT FOR FACULTY

Your leadership, words, and actions can be the catalyst that creates a collective culture where teachers and staff engage in inquiry, reflection, self-evaluation, and collaborative conversations about research-tested changes that improve teaching and learning. The seven pillars of engagement that follow can help your work with teachers as you model expectations, raise compelling questions, and nurture the professional culture needed for courageous conversations about access, equity, and change (Robb, 2022). As you move forward, here's a question to ask yourself again and again:

How am I honoring, modeling, and fostering the development of each pillar among teachers?

CHOICE

Examining materials for access and equity can present multiple opportunities for teachers to choose culturally relevant read-aloud and instructional texts that resonate with their students. In addition, teachers offer their students choices with independent reading and writing topics. As you visit classrooms, notice whether students have choices that help them invest in their learning.

TRUSTING RELATIONSHIPS

Trust does not occur by accident and develops as you interact with teachers and staff throughout school days. Evaluating the curriculum for access and equity can open the door for challenging conversations. However, when discussions value teachers' honest feedback and suggestions, they can build trust, positive relationships, and shine the spotlight on the need for integrating culturally relevant texts into the curriculum in meaningful ways.

TEAMWORK

When you foster teamwork among teachers and administrators, you enable everyone to experience and understand that the team is stronger and can accomplish more than one person working independently. Teachers can then apply teamwork experiences to their students' learning and have groups discuss culturally relevant books and videos and work on projects together.

AGENCY AND VOICE

If teachers sense or experience that there will be repercussions for honestly sharing ideas or making decisions, agency and voice will be diminished or lost. By developing a culture of shared leadership and teamwork that respects diverse ideas and opinions, you increase teachers' agency and voice, encouraging them to share thoughts about a topic and make decisions that positively impact students' learning gains.

A RISK-TAKING ENVIRONMENT

Ensuring that equity and access to culturally relevant materials is available for all students will most likely require risk-taking among teachers. Adjusting classroom libraries and integrating culturally relevant texts into daily read-alouds and instructional reading units might be challenging ideas for some or several, but it's important that teachers demonstrate their commitment to diversity.

You can model taking risks by sharing your feelings about access and equity with grade-level teams and departments. You can share honestly by saying something like: *Our schools have culturally diverse populations and we all need to collaborate to adjust available texts, materials, and curriculum to .ensure meaningful integration into lessons.* When you start the discussion in small groups, teachers feel safer asking questions and sharing their beliefs and feelings about access and equity.

COMMUNICATION

To help teachers and staff feel they're in your communication loop, it's beneficial for you to update them on school initiatives and collaborative projects as well as respond to email queries within twenty-four hours. Equally important is creating opportunities for teachers to have professional time to discuss and communicate ideas and feelings about access and equity, professional learning opportunities, curricular issues, and students' progress. As you collaborate with teachers to achieve goals, you have daily opportunities to model through words and actions how much you value communicating ideas through informal discussions and scheduled meetings.

REFLECTION

Reflection can enhance motivation and in turn increase purposeful engagement. Start with yourself and develop the habit of reflecting at the end of the day in your office and/or on your drive or walk home. Frequent reflecting enables you to share with teachers how reflection causes you to rethink ideas and engages you in exploring research and deepening your knowledge of access and equity. You can increase engagement among faculty by encouraging reflection during and near the end of meetings and then inviting teachers to share their thoughts. When you share some of your reflections and invite teachers to reflect, you're not only actively modeling but you're also offering them opportunities that can result in their reserving time for students to reflect and share.

The seven pillars present you with many opportunities to model, engage, collaborate, share leadership, and empower teachers and other school leaders. Moreover, the seven pillars are equally applicable in a classroom for any grade level. What you model consistently and with an intentional purpose will be adopted by some teachers initially, and, with your support, others will join over time.

During the pandemic, as my teachers worked on learning how to be effective virtual and hybrid facilitators, we often reflected together on the importance of choice, teamwork, and building trusting relationships for students and for us. I encouraged them to start with questions such as:

- How can choice be part of virtual and hybrid teaching and learning?
- What parts of our curriculum do we believe students should cover?
- How do we integrate independent reading and students' access to books?
- How might grading change?

Soon teachers realized they had to choose the key elements of curriculum their students needed to learn and brainstorm how students could experience these in hybrid and virtual environments. Their discussions resulted in some teachers trying *choice boards* for virtual and hybrid learners, and they quickly discovered that inviting students to choose a learning task motivated and engaged them in the task. Choice boards also supported our school's initiatives of differentiation and increased student motivation. Soon, using choice boards spread quickly among ELA and content teachers, and students were not only motivated and engaged, but they were also decision makers, selecting tasks that interested them and committing to working carefully and diligently.

Your increasing skill in professionally motivating and engaging teachers is the best resource you have to elevate the pillars and enhance learning for all students. Consider additional ways to motivate and engage teachers: new challenges to work on, article studies, and providing specific feedback when teachers transfer what adult learners are working on to student learners in your school. Additional article studies with teachers on access and equity can focus on reviewing and comparing the actual time they have during a school day to the optimal time needed. Such discussions can result in schedule changes to support and monitor students' literacy and numeracy progress and gains.

COLLECTIVE EFFICACY: PROBLEM SOLVING IN ACTION

Collective efficacy is evident when teachers see themselves as part of a student-focused team who believe in their collective ability to improve student outcomes and higher levels of achievement (Donohoo et al., 2018). Part of collective efficacy is shifting away from blaming outside factors that may be impacting student learning and instead focusing on what teachers believe they can control while students are in school. At my school, teachers repeatedly raised the need for more time for independent reading, and I agreed with their assessment. However, finding the time was a continual challenge. Teachers, the librarian, and my administrative team tried to find extra time for students to read at school as well as reach out to families to encourage reading at home. "Frustrating" is the word that can be used to describe our efforts.

Quickly, we realized what I think we all knew but didn't say: there's a lot of competition for students' time, and reading was not always the priority. My assistant principal had an idea and asked me: *What if we created time to read during the day, time that was not in our schedule?* I asked her to set up a series of five to six meetings to discuss this idea, explore options, and receive feedback from department leaders and teachers. Several weeks later, I heard a well-prepared proposal from teachers on how to find time to increase students' reading at school. The proposal opened with this claim from the "What's Hot" Report published in *ILA Today* (2020): "Inadequate access to books in families' homes is rated as the second greatest barrier to equity." Presenters pointed out that their proposed plan would ensure all students had equal access to books and opportunities to read at school, thus reducing, they hoped, the effects of the barrier ILA described.

The plan added a microblock of twenty-five minutes to each day by taking several minutes off each ninety-minute block. Committee members had surveyed all department members, and everyone agreed that a microblock for reading was the best way to increase independent reading across the school and shift away from the frustrating "we don't have time" conversations. The independent reading microblock, wedged between first and second blocks, occurred four days a week and offered all students access to books and time to read at school. Teachers reserved the fifth day for class meetings. This year teachers adjusted the focus of the fifth day: guidance counselors and teachers teamed up and led activities and discussions to build students' social-emotional learning. The strength and will of collective efficacy, combined with teachers' creative thinking, led to an outcome that benefited all students and teachers. Keep the question that follows in the forefront of your mind, as a reminder to tap into the collective efficacy of your teachers to solve problems that can seem frustrating and insurmountable.

> Are there opportunities for you to empower teacher leaders to problem-solve, explore, and discover new and sometimes novel solutions to challenges?

The creation of the microblock provided access to culturally relevant books four days week and increased equity when all students had the same twenty-five minutes to self-select and read books that interested them. When you have developed trusting relationships and collective efficacy among teachers, they will invest time and effort in exploring possible solutions to challenges. Here are two more suggestions for you to consider—suggestions that can enlarge equity while improving students' literacy skill.

- **Reading support teacher:** The addition of an extra reading class to your schedule for students who need support can be an effective way to improve their reading skill. An extra reading class can be an elective, allowing students to have their grade-level ELA class plus an additional reading class that provides support and skill development. Reading support teachers can also work with non-ELA teachers to find materials to meet students' reading needs across the curriculum, so students are reading and improving all day long (Allington, 2007).

- **Tutorial programs:** Having additional supports for students during the day and after school provide more options that would offer students extra instruction and practice. Consider creating an elective to provide specific support to small groups of students and/or after-school academic tutorials where older students assist younger students or a qualified tutor supports individuals or small groups with similar needs. Three conditions need to be in place for after-school programs to work: tutors receive payment, the school transports students home, and the tutor and classroom teacher communicate regularly.

Today, over 30 million children lack access to books in their homes, schools, and communities. These students live in high-poverty areas that lack reading materials and in many cases access to broadband. Circumstances beyond the children's control create these disparities in access and equity. Recent research shows significant disparities in the availability of books between high-income and low-income neighborhoods, even within the same city. In a high-poverty area of Washington, DC (with poverty levels above 60 percent), there is one book per 833 children (Neuman & Moland, 2019).

Books open doors to access and the expansion of equity for students, but issues such as poverty and poor health care can inhibit access and equity. However, there is much you, teachers, and staff can do by turning collaborative plans into actions when you create the conditions for change: engage in conversations with teachers; empower teachers to become agents of change for refining schedules, developing quality instruction, responding to students' needs, increasing students' access to books and learning materials; and creating a culture of high expectations that results in significant gains. When your leadership includes funding for an abundance of books and materials and scheduling that supports all students, it's possible for you to motivate and engage teachers to use instructional practices that increase access and equity as well as result in solid learning gains for all students.

HYBRID LEADERSHIP TIPS

Students in hybrid classrooms have access to books from their classroom and school libraries. However, students who choose to learn virtually have limited access to books. They can check out books from their public library if they can get there, they can find e-books on an e-platform or if their school has one, or they can find reading materials in the public domain on the Internet. Clearly, children who are in all-virtual learning in a hybrid district have limited access to books and other learning materials. Some might have limited access to the Internet. This challenge presents an opportunity to you and your teachers to find ways to get books and other materials into the hands of virtual learners.

Use the ACCESS model to collaborate with teachers and your librarian to review, evaluate, and propose various ways of bringing books and materials to virtual students. Brainstorm a list of suggestions that ensure virtual learners have access to books; discuss each one, and decide on what you, teachers, and the librarian can reasonably accomplish. Here are some actions that can ensure virtual students have materials similar to hybrid students for learning and independent reading.

- **Deliver books to students' homes:** Your librarian, literacy coach, or a lead teacher can organize a group of parent and teacher volunteers who can deliver books to students' homes and pick up completed books and materials. Schools that have a book delivery system either drive or ride bikes to destinations.
- **Have families pick up and return at school:** Via email or phone calls, let families know the day, time, and location for picking up and returning books at your school for their children. Place books and other materials in bags with the child's name printed on the outside. A staff member can monitor the pickup process to ensure it works well.
- **Create a mobile library for children in remote areas:** If your school has a small van or sports utility vehicle (SUV), fill it with books, and enlist teacher and parent volunteers to deliver and pick up to specific families. Your librarian or teachers can stock the vehicle with library books a child can check out on delivery days and at the same time return completed books. When a school doesn't own a suitable vehicle, parents might volunteer to use their SUV.

Once all students have books and materials, next steps include considering ways to engage students at school in meaningful conversations.

WHO'S DOING THE TALKING?

Whether your school is normal, hybrid, or all-virtual, students should do as much of the talking as possible. Talk is an oral text that enables students to clarify and refine their thinking (Robb, 2017). Moreover, when students write about reading in their notebooks, it's beneficial for them to discuss the issue, topic, or theme prior to writing as talk can raise new ideas and help them find text evidence to support a position (Robb, 2017).

Organize several meetings with teams and departments and invite teachers to do the following:

- Self-monitor their hybrid and/or virtual classes to determine who's doing most of the talking.

- Invite teachers to study ways to group students for discussion in class and virtually.

- Ask teachers to use inquiry and have students raise questions for discussions.

Teachers can find articles to read and discuss through an Internet search. Here are some books you can purchase for your school's professional library—books that encourage students to do most of the talking to learn and grow as critical thinkers.

BOOKS THAT ENCOURAGE STUDENTS TO DISCUSS

Hands Down, Speak Out by Kassia Wedekind and Christy Thompson, Stenhouse, 2020.

Read, Talk, Write by Laura Robb, Corwin Literacy, 2017.

Who's Doing the Talking? by Jan Burkins and Kari Yates, Stenhouse, 2019.

Equity and access to books and materials as well as high expectations will remain critical focal points for reflection and change as your school shifts to more in-person learning. To meet specific challenges, invite teachers to learn in collaborative groups and share at full faculty meetings articles that were helpful and suggestions for colleagues to integrate into their lessons.

CONSIDER THESE ACTIONS AND AIM HIGH

- Collaborate with your librarian and several ELA teachers to review school and classroom book collections and have them list specific needs.

- Commit to being a partner with teachers and other school leaders in the change process for access and equity.

- Invite teachers to share the strengths of their curricula and where improvement can be made.

- Choose three or four pillars of engagement to focus on through words and actions and encourage teachers to do the same.

- Reflect on your school schedule. Consider empowering a leader on your team to explore with teachers finding and using time to provide student supports.

- Assess your communication with faculty, students, staff and parents, list strengths plus any areas you can improve, discuss the list with other school leaders, and develop a plan for implementing changes to bring to faculty.

- Invite teachers to learn more about student-led discussions and how to pose interpretive questions that can lead to critical thinking.

- Check your budget to decide whether there's adequate funding for adding texts and materials to class and school libraries and to instructional units. If you need extra funding, meet with central office personnel to discuss this. You can also meet with the head of your parent-teacher organization to discuss raising money for access and equity.

Closing Reminder

As you review your school's mission and vision, include looking at access to culturally relevant books and materials and how teachers equitably meet the needs of all students they teach. Collaborate with teacher leaders to explore and decide on instructional changes such as differentiation and a student-centered approach to learning that can enhance teacher and student efficacy and at the same time increase growth of all students.

CHAPTER 6

Leading for Literacy

I called Jake, our division personnel director, to let him know that an English teacher was moving to another state and I would have a vacancy. As I waited for Jake to answer, I couldn't help recalling that I was losing a strong, student-focused teacher who was knowledgeable about our curriculum and able to effectively incorporate four types of reading: teacher read-alouds, instructional reading, authentic notebook writing, and independent reading. He spoke quickly and loudly: "Evan, this is no problem at all. We get tons of English applicants."

With some hesitation, I said, "Okay, you know I've worked for several years to build a very skilled team. I don't think replacing her will be that easy, but maybe I'm wrong!"

"Of course you're wrong. English teachers, dude, they're a dime a dozen. By the way, what's that four types of reading stuff you talk about all the time?"

"Never mind, I'll save the explanation for another time."

"You know, I'm sure I heard you discuss the four some-things a few times; I just can't remember it. Oh well, who won the golf tournament yesterday?"

"I didn't get a chance to watch it. I'd like to start interviews next week."

Over the next three days, my assistant principal, English department chair, and I reviewed applications and were pleased with the number of applicants. Ultimately, we selected six and arranged for three interviews per day. Prior to the first interview, we reviewed the standard questions we were to ask teacher applicants, and then we each added an extra question: *How would you instruct a novel? How does independent reading improve students' reading skill? How can you integrate reading and writing in a middle school classroom?* After the second day of interviews, we debriefed using this question: "*What are the strengths of the applicants and are there any concerns?*"

My assistant was quick to share that four applicants didn't appear knowledgeable about how to teach reading. She noted, "I get perplexed when a person has a master's degree and the best idea they share to teach a novel is round robin reading or reading it out loud to the class."

Joan, our English department chair, chimed in, "If we need to select from these interviews, Evan, you better help me find some extra mentor time, as this will be a lot of work."

"Let's go back to the applications and see if we can set up some more interviews." I suggested, trying to sound optimistic. Frankly, my worries about the applicant pool increased. Moreover, given English teachers' workloads, it would be difficult for me to ask any of them to volunteer to train a teacher with a limited knowledge of teaching reading and writing. Momentum seemed to be slipping. The three of us hoped that luck would smile on the English department by sending a skilled applicant, but we began to accept that it was more likely the new teacher would require extensive training.

Later that afternoon, my phone rang; it was our personnel director. "Didn't I tell you we had lots of applicants? Let me know which candidate you're offering the job to. I've gotta get the applicant's name to the board. Did any of them know about those two types of reading?"

"It's four types, and I've got a call on my other line."

The process of finding the right person for our teachers and students wasn't easy. We didn't find a person who was highly skilled and well trained, but we were fortunate to hire a teacher very eager and willing to learn. As I reflect, I'm lucky to have a team committed to the mentorship needed to maintain our core beliefs for teaching reading and writing. And I've come to understand that at times hiring faculty for potential instead of credentials can also work out for the team, department, and students.

DEVELOP AN EFFECTIVE READING PLAN

Effective principals elevate, support, and collaborate with teachers and also raise and discuss questions that enable faculty and them to work toward the development of initiatives to enhance learning. Literacy and leading for literacy are challenging during ideal times, but the challenges have escalated post-pandemic. Virtual learning and hybrid classrooms have increased the opportunities for some students to disengage from reading and for other students to read more than they ever have done before. The pandemic has heightened disparities among students, and having an effective reading plan can support your goal of addressing literacy disparities. A well-thought-out and well-led plan will set your school on a path to meet the needs of *all* readers, as you increase the amount of reading students complete daily and elevate the teachers' role in promoting literacy through professional learning conversations and collaborative inquiry.

A DEEP DIVE INTO THE FOUR TYPES OF READING

To lead literacy in a school, it's important to gain an understanding of what an effective literacy curriculum looks like. My experiences as a student, adult learner, and partnership with Laura Robb helped to form, shape, and now continually refine my understanding of the four types of reading that allow ELA teachers in my school to meet the literacy needs of all students.

However, my connections with school districts in and out of Virginia reveal that there's much work to do, and to that end, I've developed a list of reading practices that can't support the progress of all students—practices that still exist in many schools:

- One book for everyone in the class
- Textbooks and anthologies with selections from actual books that many students can't read
- Books read out loud by the teacher because too many students couldn't read them
- Assessments to motivate students through point accumulation and prizes
- Endless test-prep materials to prepare students to take state assessments
- Demoralizing round robin or popcorn reading

The one book or one program for all students in a class supports literacy learning of students that read near or on grade level. Above-grade-level students, though bored and unchallenged, can do the work. Developing readers, those two or more years below grade level, make little progress, and many teachers refer to them as "the low group."

I am often asked what types of reading should occur in a middle school English classroom. What is a balanced, research-tested, authentic literacy program? My answer is not that complex: Reading can and should be taught. Effective language arts curricula improve the literacy of all students. To accomplish this goal, classrooms need four types of reading:

1. Instructional interactive read-alouds
2. Instructional reading
3. Readers' notebooks
4. Independent reading

INSTRUCTIONAL INTERACTIVE READ-ALOUDS

An interactive read-aloud allows the teacher to model in a think-aloud mode how to apply a reading strategy as well as emotional reactions and posing questions. This modeling during a read-aloud builds and enlarges students' mental model of how a strategy works and what readers do while interacting with a text. For this aspect of instruction, the teacher models with a short text that matches the genre and/or theme that ties a reading unit together. Short texts can include a picture book, an excerpt from a longer text, a folk or fairy tale, myth or legend, a short short story, or an article from a magazine or newsletter. Following are six of many strategies and responses that teachers can model during interactive read-aloud lessons:

- Making inferences
- Linking literary elements to a text
- Identifying big ideas and themes
- Skimming to locate important details
- Posing questions
- Emotional responses

The interactive read-aloud is your teachers' common text. Once teachers complete the modeling over five to eight classes, they move to reading aloud from culturally diverse texts that resonate with students—texts that are enjoyable and are catalysts for meaningful discussions of topics and/or issues. Interactive read-alouds are resources that teachers can refer to while supporting students with instructional reading.

Schools Full of Readers by Laura Robb and Evan Robb (2020) has detailed information on planning and implementing lessons for the anchor text, an interactive read-aloud.

INSTRUCTIONAL READING

Instructional reading occurs during a classroom session. Students need to read materials at their instructional reading level, which is about 90–95 percent reading accuracy and about 90 percent comprehension (Fountas & Pinnell, 2009). Organizing instructional reading around a genre and theme—for example biography with a theme of obstacles—permits students to read different texts at their instructional reading levels and discuss their reading around the genre and theme. Teachers also use guided or strategic groups for instruction, and small groups of students read and learn from the same accessible text.

LITERACY LEADERSHIP TIP

Most likely, one book for all does not support the range of readers in your school's classrooms. Moreover, it's based on a false premise that all students are on the same reading level.

Instructional reading asks and guides students to apply specific strategies to texts that can improve comprehension, vocabulary, and critical thinking and foster diverse interpretations. These texts stretch students' thinking with the teacher, the expert, as a supportive guide. Reading does not exist isolated from writing, and writing about reading in readers' notebooks can be a bridge connecting reading and writing to deepen comprehension.

READERS' NOTEBOOKS

When you consider your school's writing program, it's important to understand how much daily writing students complete and whether teachers embrace the workshop model. Readers' notebooks are a place for students to write about their instructional reading and teachers' read-aloud texts. Notebook writing can flourish when teachers "cold write" and think aloud to provide students with a model of specific types of responses to texts before inviting students to write. Responses can include lists of words to describe characters' and readers' feelings, characters' personality traits, questions the text raised, predictions, application of strategies and literary elements, and notes for an analytical paragraph. Readers' notebooks represent the reading journeys students take and are often hunches that students adjust, rethink, and add text evidence in support of their interpretations.

Laura Robb recommends not grading students' notebooks or marking them up to correct grammar and punctuation (Robb, 2022). Instead, have students complete their paragraphs or writing to show how they infer, compare and contrast, visualize, and so forth on separate paper and let them know these will be graded. She also recommends that teachers keep a list of grammar and punctuation needs and turn these into mini-lessons during writing workshop.

During the reading class, students should have their headed notebooks on their desks, so they're ready to write to increase understanding. The research on writing about reading shows that students' comprehension of text they can read improves when they write.

RESEARCH ON WRITING ABOUT READING TO IMPROVE COMPREHENSION

A landmark study and meta-analysis published in 2010 by the Carnegie Corporation, *Writing to Read: Evidence for How Writing Can Improve Reading,* revealed the power of readers' notebooks and writing about reading to improve students' comprehension (Graham & Hebert, 2010). The recommendations that Steve Graham and Michael Hebert suggest are the kinds of writing they want students to complete:

- Reading responses expressing personal reactions to a text
- Interpreting themes and big ideas using text evidence as support
- Summaries
- Lists of words that describe characters' personality traits and readers' emotional reactions to events, settings, decisions
- Notes about a text
- Posing questions about the text and answering them

When teachers ask students to write about conversations after a pair-share or small-group discussion, they are providing the practice of clarifying ideas needed to write about reading. In 2015, Steve Graham completed another study of the benefits of writing about reading with Katherine Harris and Tanya Santangelo. The three researchers found that when students write about material they can read and understand, their comprehension of that text can rise by 24 percent (Graham et al., 2015).

Clearly, teachers reading aloud, instructional reading that meets students where they are, and writing about reading boost students' expertise and skill. Now, add independent reading, the practice that can move students forward quickly, and you can see the power behind the four kinds of reading.

INDEPENDENT READING

Students should always carry a book they are reading independently, so if they complete the class work, they can read. By encouraging them to read accessible books they select on topics they love and want to know more about, teachers develop students' motivation to read! Review and share the "15 Benefits of Independent Reading" (page 171, in the Appendix) with your staff and families, so they can see the value of independent reading and how it impacts students' learning (Robb et al., 2020). Getting hung up on how to hold students accountable is counterproductive. Remember, enthusiastic readers of any age do not summarize every chapter they read in a journal. Neither do you!

Students should complete twenty to thirty minutes of independent reading a night for their main homework assignment. If you're on a block schedule, set aside two days a week for students to complete independent reading at school. If you have 90 to 120 minutes for reading and writing daily, then independent reading should occur every day. Independent reading of self-selected books is an important use of classroom time because it's the practice that builds students' background knowledge, vocabulary, literary tastes, reading identities, and a lifelong love of reading. When students read, the teacher can read part of the time, which communicates a great message to students: adults read independently, too! Equally important during this time, teachers can have a few brief conferences with students about their reading.

For students to make significant learning gains, they should be engaged in practices that are far better than popcorn reading or reading an entire book aloud to students because they can't read it. Including the four types of reading can serve as the framework for your reading curriculum, bringing balance to your school's reading curriculum and at the same time motivate and engage students. As you develop a reading initiative that includes the four types of reading, you'll participate in and create teacher buy-in as well as find funds for books and professional learning opportunities.

As leader of your school's reading initiative, reflect on the collaborations with teachers that need to occur to enhance their understanding of the benefits of the four types of reading and increase learning gains for all students.

CHARACTERISTICS OF LITERACY LEADERS

Literacy leaders are knowledgeable about research, research-tested practices, and how a partnership between research and best instructional practices can improve reading. Most important, as a literacy leader you communicate ideas, collaborate and seek opportunities to learn alongside teachers, listen to understand, and are open to feedback and new ideas. Highly visible throughout the day, you continually spend time in classrooms, discuss literacy with teachers and students, attend school events, and consistently cultivate a culture that celebrates and promotes literacy. The principal sets the tone and climate in a school through interactions and support and by communicating high expectations for all learners. Set aside time to read and self-evaluate the characteristics of a literacy leader listed below and then create a list of your own strengths and needs.

- Collectively establishes a culture of high expectations
- Promotes diversity, inclusivity, and equity
- Encourages instructional risk-taking
- Helps teachers view failures as information that can help them refine present instructional practices and try new ones, always with the goal of improving instruction

- Believes in sharing leadership with teachers
- Communicates and maintains high standards for professionalism
- Works closely with the school librarian and language arts teachers to create literacy goals
- Commits to learning about researched-tested best practices for effective instruction
- Makes professional learning an ongoing priority and actively participates

Collaborating with teachers to develop a schoolwide reading initiative enables you to pinpoint your school's strengths and needs. The seven indicators that follow can support you and faculty as you set literacy priorities and develop a plan.

IMPLEMENTING A READING INITIATIVE USING SEVEN INDICATORS

The success of a reading initiative requires planning, collaboration, and at times a cultural shift. The first step is to visit ELA classrooms to observe whether the four types of reading are part of instruction. Then, begin informal conversations with individual teachers to understand their teaching and learning strengths, challenges, and resources they need.

To stir reflection, a question follows the description of each indicator. Reserve time so you can think of each question independently and then collaborate with ELA and content teachers to discuss one indicator at a time. Doing this can enable you and teachers to create a list of priorities for your reading initiative. For example, if teachers have forty minutes a day for reading and writing, a top priority would be to study and adjust your schedule so that teachers can include the four types of reading into each class and develop students' critical and analytical thinking skills.

SCHEDULES

A schedule alone does not create readers, but skilled teachers do, and they require enough time to focus on literacy effectively. Typically, school schedules range from seven or eight periods a day to blocks of time every day or every other day. The ideal schedule for your school is the schedule that allows teachers to meet the needs of students using the four types of reading. However, creating a schedule is not always possible, and changes to schedules can impact other class offerings and staffing. If your teachers have a genuine concern about the schedule's limitation, consider a meeting with you, teachers, and central office personnel to discuss their scheduling concerns.

Question: *Does your school's schedule provide enough time for teachers to incorporate the four types of reading?*

CRITICAL THINKING AND PROBLEM SOLVING

Instruction in ELA and content classrooms should provide students with multiple opportunities to observe as teachers model and think aloud the process of critical thinking and problem solving. As students build their mental models of the process, they can examine and analyze information from teachers' read-alouds and instructional and independent reading. Students can use writing about reading and student-led conversations to critically analyze, reflect on, and evaluate information, so they can separate faulty conclusions from sound ones and identify misleading or false information, always citing text evidence and data to support their conclusions.

Question: *Are teachers modeling and thinking aloud to explicitly show students how to think analytically and critically and solve problems?*

HIGH-LEVEL THINKING STRATEGIES

Strategies such as visualizing, inferring, comparing and contrasting, and posing interpretive questions encourage students to think deeply about information and facts to determine their level of recall, and deepen their understanding by moving beyond the facts. Too often, reading instruction focuses only on factual recall instead of inviting students to find multiple interpretations supported with text evidence. When my daughter was in sixth grade, she missed a question on Natalie Babbitt's *Tuck Everlasting* (1975) test asking the color of the stranger's suit. It was yellow, but there is much more to the book than the question she answered incorrectly.

Question: *Are teachers integrating high-level reading strategies into their units of study and inviting students to explore and practice finding multiple interpretations of texts?*

CHOICES FOR STUDENTS

Effective ELA classrooms offer students choices in independent and instructional reading and writing topics, audience, and genres. Choice not only invests students in their reading and writing, but it also leads to independence as students become more and more responsible for their learning.

Question: *How are teachers in your school incorporating student choice into instructional and independent reading as well as in writing tasks?*

AUTHENTIC WRITING

Writing is a skill, and skills improve when students practice. Many schools need to increase the amount of time students write each day in ELA classrooms and across the school. "Most writing researchers and teachers of note now advise that students should write between 30 and 60 minutes every day. The logic behind this is that nothing is more important for writing development than putting in the hours defining and refining one's voice, organizing and reorganizing one's thoughts, and learning how words spill out of one's head and onto the page" (Johnson, 2017). In addition to choosing the topics and writing stories, poems, articles, plays, and so on, students' reading comprehension improves when they write about reading in notebooks (see pages 119–120).

Question: *How often are students writing in ELA classrooms, and how much of the writing connects to what students are reading?*

CONVERSATIONS AND DISCUSSIONS

Discussions are usually teacher-led and students raise hands waiting to be called on to respond to a teacher-made question. Conversations ask students to listen carefully and respond to what a peer says without raising a hand; they are usually student led and use questions that students raise. Literary conversations about books and other texts occur in ELA classes, but conversations can also occur in content subjects when talk centers on texts related to specific topics and issues. Conversations and discussions invite students to interact with texts and can create a shared literacy culture (Robb, 2017).

Question: *What would literary conversations look like in an ELA classroom? What are the roles of students and teachers?*

CONFERRING WITH STUDENTS

Conferring can be between a teacher and one student, a teacher and a small group, or student partners exploring similar issues and topics. Teachers hold brief—no more than five minutes—one-on-one meetings with students to learn about their reading and writing lives and attitudes as well as to observe and support students' growth as readers and writers. Effective conferring allows teachers to honor and build on a student's strengths in order to support specific needs. It's helpful for teachers to keep dated notes of conferences so they can monitor students' progress and review specific details and observations to make informed instructional decisions (Yates & Nosek, 2018).

Question: *Is conferring occurring on a regular basis in ELA classrooms in your school, and what are other students doing when the teacher is conferring with an individual or small group?*

As you and teachers take time to discuss the seven indicators and the questions, invite them to reflect on the kinds of professional learning they'll need. Then, ask teachers to take on leadership roles and develop professional learning experiences for each indicator that requires additional study.

PROFESSIONAL LEARNING LEADS TO GROWTH IN STUDENTS' LEARNING

For teachers to learn and practice instructional moves that positively impact students' rate of growth, designing a professional learning menu that offers teachers choices of groups that meet simultaneously taps into the diverse learning needs of your teachers. For example, you might organize two groups meeting at the same time—one on conferring and a second on readers' notebooks and writing about reading. Depending on the background knowledge of your teachers, you might add a third group studying student-led conversations or high-level thinking strategies.

QUESTIONS TO PONDER BEFORE GETTING STARTED

The questions that follow can enable you, teachers, and your school's librarian to set priorities, consider the funding needed for purchases, and decide on a menu of professional learning opportunities that meet your teachers' needs.

- Which indicators are strongest and which require immediate attention?

- What do you and your teachers think the best starting point or points are?

- What materials do teachers need: additional texts for interactive read-alouds, a document camera, and bookcases?

- How many additional books for classroom libraries and for instructional reading texts does each teacher require? Do students need readers' notebooks?

- How much funding do teachers require immediately? How much funding do you need to set aside for books and materials annually?

Once you and teachers have committed to changes in your literacy curriculum, it's important to communicate these to families.

KEEP FAMILIES IN THE LOOP

Keep families informed about changes in your literacy curriculum, so you can explain how they can support your reading initiative at home and by volunteering to help in the library and with special projects and events. A video from you detailing the goals and benefits as well as updates from teachers and your librarian in electronic newsletters and email blasts can continually keep families in the loop. This can result in families feeling that they are a valued part of your school community and will also prepare them for changes in virtual and hybrid learning.

HYBRID LEADERSHIP TIPS

Whether students are hybrid or all-virtual, it's important for them to experience the four types of reading. As you review the suggestions that follow, remember that volume in reading matters for all students—volume ensures they're practicing enough to make significant reading gains.

Teacher Read-Alouds

I recommend that when teachers use interactive read-alouds as an instructional tool they complete the read-aloud in person during a hybrid class or online, so students can be part of the process. Teachers can also create a video of the high points of the instructional read-aloud so students can rewatch to deepen their understanding. Read-alouds that are a catalyst for students discussing a topic should also be in person. However, read-alouds for students' pleasure and enjoyment can be asynchronous and accessed anytime by students or within the guidelines of a listening schedule that teachers post.

Instructional Reading

For instructional reading to support the skill and progress of all students, texts must meet them where they are to move them forward. This means that teachers organize students into online and/or in-person reading groups or develop a reading workshop that has books on a genre and theme that meet the range of instructional reading levels in their classes. Your librarian can help teachers find books in the school's library, and teachers can find additional appropriate books in their classroom libraries as well as in colleague's libraries. Hybrid students can choose their books for an instructional reading workshop at school. Teachers can have students learning virtually pick up books at school or books can be delivered (see pages 108–109 in Chapter 5 for suggestions).

Independent Reading

Choice is really important for independent reading, and it's important that you ensure teachers are modeling and thinking aloud to show students how they choose books. You can suggest that teachers post the chart on a wall or bulletin board or give a

(Continued)

copy to students as a resource. Students learning virtually can choose e-books if these are available, and/or they can visit their public library if parents can drive them there or if they can walk. It's also possible for you to ask teachers to create independent reading book bags and have them picked up at school or delivered to students' homes. Ask students to keep a list of the books that they've read or abandoned on the form in the Appendix on page 176. You can suggest to teachers they have students complete a short book talk each month. Book talks are an excellent way for students to learn about books their peers have read and enjoyed.

Readers' Notebooks

Whether hybrid or all-virtual, it's best to use online journals for notebooks. This allows teachers to access and read specific entries, and it allows students to share entries with classmates. It's still possible for teachers to model what a notebook entry should include by writing under an online document camera that many platforms have. It's important for students to watch teachers write, think aloud, and edit notebook entries before they write.

HOW TO CHOOSE A "GOOD FIT" BOOK: TEACHERS

Choosing a "good fit" book: what teachers can do and a chart for students to use (Robb, 2022).

- Think aloud to show what happens when you choose a book that's too difficult: can't say many words, don't know many word meanings, and can't recall details.

- Think aloud when you find a "good fit" book: it's easy to read and enjoyable and you can retell.

- Model using suggestions from the list below.

- Keep modeling and emphasize that independent reading should be enjoyable and easy.

- Reassure students that they are safe selecting a book that looks easy in your class. Explain that the more they read, the faster they'll improve.

HOW TO CHOOSE A "GOOD FIT" BOOK: STUDENTS

- Look for books on topics and genres that interest you.

- Study the front cover illustration and read the information on the back cover or the inside cover flap.

- Think of books you've read and enjoyed. Is the topic, genre, or author similar?

- Look at and enjoy the illustrations or photographs.

- Ask a friend to recommend a book.

- Ask your teacher to recommend a book.

- Read the chapter titles in the table of contents and ask yourself, *Does this interest me?*

- Take a test drive and read two to three pages or the first chapter. Can you retell key points?

CONSIDER THESE ACTIONS AND AIM HIGH

- Meet with department chairs and explore how teachers use the four types of reading, and then discuss strengths and needs.

- Invite your librarian and/or reading resource teacher to meet with ELA teachers and discuss their needs for interactive read-alouds. Have the librarian follow up with suggestions.

- Ask teachers to assess their classroom library needs—print and e-books—and let you know what's needed immediately so you can support them.

- Collaborate with ELA teachers to explore their instructional reading needs and whether there's funding for additional books.

- Collaborate with teachers to compare your reading curriculum to the seven indicators and develop a list of priorities.

- Create with teachers a plan for professional learning and decide if everyone needs to study all the topics or if you can create a menu that has two to three topics available simultaneously.

- Ask teachers to volunteer to organize and facilitate a professional learning group and gather materials for the study. Make sure you meet with each teacher leader to review materials, time frames, and expectations.

- Invite a group of teachers to investigate the different types of conferring they can do with students and report back to you and colleagues with information and a list of books and articles.

Closing Reminder

It's important to remember that one book, one basal program, or computer programs that promises to meet students' needs with short texts and frequent quizzes can't meet the needs of a diverse student population. Instead, with your teachers, develop a literacy initiative and curriculum that invests in ongoing professional learning and sets aside annual funding for culturally relevant books for classroom libraries, instructional reading units, and your school's media center!

CHAPTER 7

Leading for Numeracy

"Our data is not accurate," Robert, the math department chair, told me.

"What's the issue leading to these inaccuracies?"

"Evan, central office asked us to give a math screening assessment to all students, but half of them are virtual, and teachers can't assess those that never login."

"I understand. You need the data to make placement recommendations for next year."

"At best, the data we already have shows some gaps we would not normally see; at worst, the gaps are significant."

The question this conversation raises is, *How can you, the leader of your school, address this issue?*

My department chair and I faced a challenge all schools will cope with post-pandemic: students have gaps in their math learning, and the student placements that teachers recommend can impact scheduling. However, the challenge is how principals lead staff, students, and families away from a fix-it mentality and deficit model that can cause diminished self-confidence and math anxiety among students to identifying and building on their strengths. Though math anxiety is nothing new for students or their parents, the leadership of school divisions, principals, and teacher leaders have an important post-pandemic decision to make regarding students' motivation to learn: reduce or increase math anxiety.

It would be unusual to move through the pandemic and not read or hear discussions about learning loss or learning slide. These deficit model terms don't accurately describe what occurred during a year of virtual and hybrid learning. First, no child loses past learning that can be reclaimed through review. Students who didn't have access to the Internet and a computer or handheld device and those who didn't attend virtual classes missed math instruction, and the research of Northwest Evaluation Association (NWEA) verifies this. This year NWEA tested 4.4 million students and found that compared with last year there was a 5–10 percentile drop in math scores, with the larger drop in Grades 3 to 6 (Fensterwald, 2020). These results don't include the 30 percent of students who had no math instruction due to a lack of Internet access and a computer or by choice never attended virtual classes.

As more students return to schools, instruction will shift away from virtual and hybrid models toward in-person learning five days a week. The changes teachers and students experienced during the year of COVID-19 open the door for conversations and reflection about math instruction, including your school's strengths and challenges. First, to identify students' math skill level, encourage your teachers to use formative assessments, observations, and brief conferences that enable teachers to determine students' strengths and needs and also inform their instructional moves. Next, reserve time to check in with your math teachers through conversations and informal observations, and ask teachers to share any data reviews. Doing this provides you with the information that not only lets you know where students are with numeracy and materials teachers might need but also enables you to partner with teachers in support of students. Your post-pandemic instructional leadership matters and can provide the support your teachers need to move all students forward with math learning.

When students return full time to your school, instructional leadership will fall into two camps: the deficit and asset-based camp. There's a decision you'll have to make before you collaborate with teachers to develop a math success plan—a decision that can affect the learning of every student: which model will you embrace—deficit or asset?

Which model will you embrace—deficit or asset?

POSITIVE LEADERSHIP GOALS: ASSET-BASED VERSUS DEFICIT-BASED

My hope is that you'll adopt an asset-based approach to leading numeracy in your school. An asset-based model builds on students' potential by focusing on the strengths of students. In contrast, a deficit model focuses on students' weaknesses. If schools focus too heavily on students' weaknesses post-pandemic, they risk becoming remediation hubs whose primary goal is to "fix" students, often increasing math anxiety, a burden that students can carry for years.

Progress can occur and students' self-confidence can grow with an asset-based model as teachers scaffold and support, organize peer partnerships that encourage students to guide and help one another, and as you find time in the schedule for students to receive extra help in small groups. Avoid putting the content before the child.

Instead, consider how your leadership with teachers, students, and families can build upon students' strengths and support their learning needs to increase their understanding of math concepts and problem solving.

FIVE BELIEFS THAT ADDRESS NUMERACY LEARNING

The numeracy challenges that you face are unique to this post-pandemic time. However, what isn't new is how you support teachers by building trusting relationships and inviting them to collaborate to explore ways to ensure that every student progresses with math learning. Remember, education publishers will tempt you with quick-fix solutions, but be cautious about programs that overpromise and appear too good to be effective. What works, you might wonder? You and your math teachers hold the answer: clear instructional expectations, schedule adjustments, and discussing which teachers' materials they need can lead to developing a plan that meets the unique needs of your students. Build on your math team's leadership, your teacher's vision that inspires their desire to learn in order to help every child make progress, and gradually, you'll see that students' knowledge of numeracy will improve. To accomplish this ambitious goal, reflect on five beliefs based on the Council of the Great Schools (2020) and consider how you can further empower teachers so that the five beliefs guide your school's math instruction.

GRADE-LEVEL CONTENT AND APPROPRIATE CHALLENGES FOR STUDENTS

The temptation for many schools will be to increase the amount of assessments students take when they return to school. This type of thinking can set up a deficit model as teachers identify students' weaknesses and then provide remediation. Consider shelving the immediate assessments and have teachers start with grade-level curriculum using formative assessments to monitor students' progress and provide scaffolding to those who need it. Support can come from the teacher, peer partnerships, or heterogeneous teams of students collaborating to learn concepts and solve problems. When students return to school, instead of starting the year by taking assessments, invite your teachers to create a math learning community by building trusting relationships and engaging them in learning math.

DEEPER INSTRUCTION

It is given that gaps in math will exist at your school, but many students will arrive ready to learn grade-level math curricula. The conversation you can have with teachers should be less about closing gaps and more about what specific curriculum is a priority for deeper learning. Deeper learning requires teachers to review instructional methods and engage in professional learning focused on the content students need to learn as they advance through the math curriculum. Prioritizing content can shift teaching from "just in case" teaching where all missed curriculum is retaught whether or not all students need reteaching to "just in time" instruction that meets students' identified needs based on ongoing formative assessments. Station learning is an excellent strategy for meeting the diversity of needs among students, as it offers teachers time to support small groups, meet the needs of students who'd benefit from extra practice, and those ready for enrichment (see the Appendix, page 165, for more on organizing station learning).

INCLUSIVITY

Equity and access should guide your math curriculum. Many students in your district and across the country have been disproportionately impacted by the pandemic because they couldn't or didn't attend virtual classes. Your leadership can narrow these disparities, and this will be your challenge in a post-pandemic world. Your school should be a place where disparities decrease, and now is the ideal time to review equity in your school, including how organizing instruction with the well-intentioned goal of helping some students may have separated them throughout the school year from the better experiences and opportunities others have. Specific to math, multiple tracked courses for a grade level may create disparities in instruction, opportunity, and inclusion. Collaborate with your math teachers to develop scheduling adjustments and strategies that enable teachers to meet the diverse needs of all students.

OVERASSESSMENT

It's fine to assess students with division assessments several weeks after school begins, but not the moment students return to school. Students need time to adjust to school, reconnect with friends, build a community of math learners, understand teachers' expectations, and, most important, enjoy coming to school.

Assessing students' level of understanding works best when it's holistic and includes formative assessments, conferring, teacher-created summative assessments, and standardized assessments. Instead of over-relying on mandated state testing, using diverse assessments better informs teachers' instructional moves and decisions, professional collaboration, reflection, and conversations on understanding data and using the information to guide instruction. In addition, when you remind teachers to also consider the unique person behind a set of assessments by sharing stories about a child that can deepen understanding and empathy, your teachers can combine studying data with students' specific qualities that contribute to their motivation to learn math.

A STRONG COMMUNITY

The word *relationships* can seem overused, but every successful classroom and school has this in common: positive, trusting relationships. A bonded school community with a positive culture can develop and flourish with your leadership when you and teachers collaborate to enhance relationships with each other, students, and families. Students', teachers', and staffs' social and emotional needs should be your focal point as you build community in your school. To move forward with creating a strong and dedicated community, continue to focus on relationships and encourage your teachers to always put students' emotional needs in front of content. As you develop a schoolwide community of learners, set aside time to collaborate with teachers on studying your math curriculum and developing numeracy initiatives.

COMPARTMENTALIZED OR INTEGRATED MATH UNITS

Often, the content students experience in math is compartmentalized into units—a fraction unit, a percent unit, computation units, solving word-problem units; this way of organizing math curricula has existed for many years. This strategy can limit students' long-term recall of math operations already studied as they move forward and focus only on a new operation. Spiraling back and continually reviewing past units can improve retention of facts and concepts. Equally important for students' recall of math operations is inviting teachers to frame lessons that show connections between addition and multiplication, subtraction and division, and fractions and percents (Pearce, 2018).

However, once students solidly understand the concepts behind math operations, they can apply their knowledge to an integrated math curriculum. Simply put, an integrated math curriculum enables students to make math connections across disciplines and to real-life problems such as measuring rainfall over a period of time, or using math to analyze the results of a survey on screen time that students developed, as well as calculating the amount of carpeting to cover a classroom or another school area. Forging math connections enables students to experience the relevance of math to other disciplines and to school, home, community, and global problems (Drake & Burns, 2004).

Through positive, trusting relationships, you've developed grade-level and department teams that collaborate and connect to learn, study curriculum, and find ways to support students and one another. To build math relevance among students, invite all teachers to generate an abundance of cross-disciplinary ideas that include math and invite students to apply math to diverse problems and situations—moving beyond memorizing math facts.

Next, take some time to reflect on your school's math curriculum and your role in shifting away from a compartmentalized curriculum toward an integrated curriculum. As you and teachers team up to develop a math initiative for your school, invite them to discuss the benefits of bringing relevance to their math curriculum through integration and connections—benefits such as increased student engagement and investment in applying math to other subjects and real-life issues.

STARTING THE INITIATIVE

When organizing numeracy initiatives, you might consider including reading teachers to gain their support and possibly develop a cross-curricular mini-unit that focuses on reading and analyzing word problems as well as writing surveys that work. This connection can start a meaningful collaboration between math and ELA teachers. In addition, it will benefit students' reading and analysis of word problems as well as their ability to determine what they're solving for and select the data from the problem that supports their solution.

Consider how you might bridge connections between ELA teachers and math teachers for the benefit of students.

READING AND ANALYZING WORD PROBLEMS

I have often heard teachers express concerns that students could do the math, but they lacked the reading, analytical, and organizational skills needed to unpack complex word problems. When you collaborate with math and ELA teachers to identify the skills students require to solve word problems, you can understand the ways that ELA teachers can support their math colleagues. Figure 7.1 lists the reading and special thinking skills students need to meet the challenges of solving word problems. The chart also shows the mix of math and literacy skills, and the connections between both subjects.

FIGURE 7.1 • Commonalities Between Math and Literacy

MATH	LITERACY
Read for and circle math terms that identify the math computation needed to solve the problem: sum, difference, product, divided by, half, percent, total, less than, greater than, etc.	Read and note words and phrases revealing characters' feelings, personality, or words that are key details for understanding information.
Identify type of problem: one step or multiple steps; problems specific to algebra, geometry, etc.	
Pull out the facts stated in the problem and key math terms, such as percent, angle, circumference, vertices, etc.	Use facts and details in a text to infer, visualize, compare/contrast.
Visualize and draw the given facts. Practice doing this eventually leads to students visualizing in their mind.	Visualize and draw the setting, a conflict, what a character looks like.
State in your own words what the problem asks you to find or solve.	State in your own words the theme or big ideas.
Decide which information you need to solve the problem.	Determine essential from non-essential information.
Test you answer to see if it makes sense in relation to what you are solving for.	Test your conclusions to see if they grow out of text details and inferences.

The chart reflects that so much of solving word problems has to do with students' reading. You can suggest options to math and literacy teachers committed to teaming up and supporting students: ELA teachers can present a series of short (about ten to fifteen minutes) lessons in the math class and find a sub to cover their class, or the literacy and math teacher can plan a mini-course that the ELA teachers implement in their class and the math teacher can reinforce and refer to while students solve word problems. Continual practice, starting with easy problems to build students' confidence and gradually moving to complex problems, is an excellent way to improve students' ability to solve word problems.

PROBLEM SOLVING AND MAKING MATH CONNECTIONS

Solving word problems invites students to apply their knowledge of math operations. It's a reading and decision-making process that asks them to analyze, think, select, and check to ensure their answer makes sense. To increase students' problem-solving skill, discuss with teachers the gradual release model described by Pearson et al. (1983) Their model aligns with Lev Vygotsky's zones of proximal development—students' learning zone where with the support of a teacher or peer, they can understand and apply the process of solving math word problems (1978). At first, teachers model the process by thinking aloud and writing under a document camera or on large chart paper. Next, teachers organize teams of three to four students who collaborate to solve, support one another, and share their reasoning with the class. Then, move to partners collaborating and finally to students working independently. Once students can unpack and solve word problems, encourage your teachers to meet and discuss the possibility of integrating math into other disciplines.

Reflect on this question: Is your school teaching the process of problem solving or assuming that with minimal guidance students can figure it out?

CONNECTING MATH TO OTHER DISCIPLINES

You can schedule and attend a few meetings with math, science, history or social studies, and geography teachers, so they can discuss possible themes and concepts in their subjects that include math. Avoid forcing integration and know that sometimes connections can occur between math and more than one other subject. However, start small for success by connecting one discipline with math and encourage teachers to volunteer to partner and plan with a colleague from a different discipline. Volunteering for this next step in making math connections shows your respect for teachers' risk-taking levels and ensures that pairs who volunteer will invest in their project. Based on my experiences, here are suggestions for teachers to develop cross-discipline projects that matter and work!

- **Plan:** Decide the content, how much time you'll need, whether you'll teach separately and meet frequently, or whether you'll combine classes and team-teach, or a combination of both.

- **Discuss with students:** The topic or theme, your goals, and invite them to turn-and-talk to discuss their suggestions for collaborating and possible projects. Integrate students' ideas into your plans.

- **Have frequent check-ins:** Schedule regular meetings to adjust plans based on what's working and students' feedback.

- **Debrief:** Do this together and with students to identify what worked and what can be improved.

POSSIBLE INTEGRATED INTERDISCIPLINARY PROJECTS

The following suggestions invite students to use their math knowledge to apply concepts and organize information that can result in deepening their understanding of math and information in a different discipline.

- **Math and science:** Atoms, ions, and the periodic table and math operations with positive and negative numbers; states of matter and linear equations; the planets, types of orbits, geometric figures
- **Math and social studies:** Greek architecture and proportions; exploration, wars, expansion and translating to math by developing charts, graphs, and tables
- **Math and geography:** Climate change and calculations that show and predict the rate of melting glaciers and icecaps; differences between weather and climate; how scientists calculate climate; rainfall and implications for farming; graphs and tables that organize rainfall; drawing conclusions

---

By inviting teachers to share their project as it unfolds during full faculty or team meetings, you can bring others on board. This method takes more time, but it increases an understanding of the investment teachers made to those who remain on the sidelines and offers and honors choice. It also reveals your respect for differences among teachers and recognizes that some need more time to take risks and join.

Once most math teachers have embraced cross-disciplinary learning, you can invite them to discuss project-based learning that links math to school, community, and real-world problems. For example, a town or school wants to build a playground for young children, and they need to know: how much land to set aside; how much space each item needs, the cost of items and installing them, and a to-scale blueprint that shows what the playground will look like. Project-based learning resonates with students when it links to a need in your school and/or surrounding community. Therefore, the ideas generated by your teachers will be unique to your area.

PROJECT-BASED LEARNING AND MATH INTEGRATION

You might have to organize groups to collaborate to learn more about project-based learning and create a book and article study so teachers enhance their background knowledge and understand how to plan these projects. Always have teachers volunteer for this step, allowing some to become experienced experts who can mentor colleagues in need of support when they take the plunge.

Whether your teachers' focus is the basics of math, word problems, interdisciplinary learning or project-based learning, they will have students who require additional math support and interventions. By collaborating with your math teachers to learn the kinds of interventions students need, you'll be in a position to support them by discussing schedule needs, providing professional learning opportunities, and funding materials.

A MENU OF POSSIBLE MATH INTERVENTIONS

Most teachers I have known over my career have intervention strategies in place for their classrooms. At times, I have known teachers who team with colleagues to share intervention ideas and work together. The best model for effective interventions is through determining interventions by department, for this creates more equity, as each department continually studies students' needs. If interventions are specific to certain teachers, some students may receive more support than others, and that's not equity, nor is it fair.

I suggest you work with your departments to start the process and share, collaborate, and create agreed-upon tiers of interventions used by all teachers in the department. Have discussions with teachers, explore your school's interventions, data that may support effectiveness, and what triggers intervention. Most often, intervention is what teachers do when learning is not occurring, and I don't argue with this definition. However, consider that intervention can also occur when students demonstrate a higher mastery of content. This intervention, often called enrichment, is essential to keeping in the conversation as you work with teachers to best meet the needs of *all* students. In addition, interventions can range from purchased programs to teacher-created interventions, from structured Response to Intervention programs to schools without RTI. But either way, students will need intervention, and balanced intervention is usually the best way to go. The first step is to move past deficit model interventions and toward interventions that provide a more targeted and timely approach to meeting student needs.

TRADITIONAL INTERVENTIONS

- Up to each teacher…
- Remedial classes
- Summer school

- "Alternative" education
- Retention
- Do nothing at all

If some of your teachers still embrace a few of these interventions, it's time to help them move forward—you can do this through collaborative discussions of articles that focus on interventions that support students' needs.

EFFECTIVE INTERVENTION

Effective intervention starts with formative assessment, knowing which students can move on, need extra practice, or would benefit from intervention. These assessments include teachers' observations of students during a mini-lesson, while students' practice, and noting the questions they raise. In addition, teachers can review written class work, quizzes, and exit slips where students complete, independently, a task practiced during a core class, as well as observe students while they complete a series of interventions.

Think of interventions in terms of two levels: the first level is the core curriculum of the classroom teacher who has the most direct impact on students' learning. The next level includes math specialists or interventionists, counselors, and other math department teachers. Encourage classroom teachers to discuss and strategize to build a menu of interventions they can use when a student needs support. These interventions can include phone calls to parents, parent and student meetings, lunch or after-school support sessions, reteaching, and redo opportunities.

Formalizing math interventions can also include after-school support, elective pullouts, and additional meetings or contacts with families so they learn how to help their child. Counselors can also be a layer of support, especially for students experiencing math anxiety and/or with low self-confidence. Some schools have support electives available for students who need even more help during the day.

There isn't one way to create an effective intervention plan for your school as plans depend on the population your school serves. It's important for you and teachers to continually revisit your plan to make adjustments and changes in order to support students' math growth. When considering an intervention, you need to ensure that the foundations of your core curriculum and formative assessments are strong in your school. If they're not, a school can spend time intervening when intervening may not be needed. It's important to note that you can't fix the walls of a house if the foundation has cracks. So, let's explore a solid math foundation: good instruction.

DIFFERENTIATED INSTRUCTION: A MENU OF INTERVENTION MOVES

To meet the needs of all students, try differentiation using a variety of instructional moves. Post-pandemic, you might find that students' math needs are greater and require more intervention.

Throughout this book, I have referred to the power of self-efficacy and collective efficacy: when teachers have a wide range of skills to teach students and embrace a belief that not everyone learns the same way, learning increases. When you and math teachers believe that students can learn and move forward with differentiated instruction and formative assessment, you raise the bar for all students! What follows is a list of eight instructional practices that should occur in your school's core math curriculum and can also be used by math support teachers. Remember to revisit the list with teachers and have collaborative discussions that bring instructional practices as well as access and equity into the conversation.

EIGHT INSTRUCTIONAL MOVES FOR DIFFERENTIATING MATH INSTRUCTION

This is not an exhaustive list but includes practices that my teachers find effective because they provide a mental model for students and also allow teachers to offer extra practice and enrich students' learning. For more detailed information on some of these interventions, see pages 173–175 in the Appendix.

1. **Teacher modeling and think-aloud:** When teachers think aloud and show students how to solve a problem, they enable students to construct a mental model of the process and can guide them toward the deeper thinking needed to understand relationship of math operations to problem solving.

2. **Guided math small-group instruction:** When teachers work with students in smaller groups, they recognize that some students may need additional instruction, different instruction, or reteaching to learn a skill or concept and enrichment (Sammons & Boucher, 2017). Guided math groups can meet the diverse needs of all students, and through a rotation model teachers can support students who require intervention, enrichment, and groups benefiting from extra practice (see pages 173–174 in the Appendix for more on organizing guided math groups). Guided practice groups can occur for an entire semester or for one to three weeks, depending on students' needs and teachers' schedules.

3. **Conferring and connecting:** Short, one-to-one discussions about math can enhance a student's understanding and allow teachers to identify roadblocks to a student's comprehension of a process. Conferring also expands opportunities for teachers to identify students who can support one another in partnerships or small groups.

4. **Personalizing learning:** Personalizing learning can use data analysis and formative assessments to guide developing instruction that meets the specific needs of each student. Teachers use their knowledge of a student's needs to create a math support plan that can include using technology and/or learning with a peer partner.

5. **Blended learning:** The best classrooms will find balance between online learning and in-class learning. Post-pandemic, teachers many feel, and I would agree, that students have had too much screen time. Where is the balance? What is right for your teachers and parents? This is an important conversation for you to have.

6. **Station learning:** This is a great strategy for differentiating and for enabling students to apply skills. Station learning allows teachers to work with a small group while other students complete enrichment and extra practice (see the Appendix, page 165).

7. **Flipping the classroom:** A different way to think about and plan instruction is to have students complete a lesson at home by following a video you create and/or completing readings. In class, students practice in front of you and pose questions, allowing you time to support them and grasp their level of understanding.

8. **Choice boards:** The teacher posts a list of learning experiences for students to choose from on a whiteboard or large chart paper. This can be a strong

differentiation activity for students and a collaborative opportunity for teachers as they consider how to empower students and develop agency through choice.

These eight instructional moves can increase teacher ownership, student engagement, and confidence, as well as disrupt one teaching-and-learning method for all students. When you encourage math teachers to offer experiences that enable students to apply math operations to other subjects and projects, you help them aim high and steadily increase students' math learning gains.

TIME IS A THIEF

Since time during a school day is finite, you can tap into teachers' creativity to adjust time so that teachers can provide students with support and interventions. Here are some suggestions:

- **Microblocks:** You can create a microblock of twenty to thirty minutes by taking a few minutes off each block or class period. To reach all math learners, micro-blocks can include interventions, extra practice, and enrichment.

- **Electives:** You can explore removing an elective or creating a new elective so teachers have more time to support students' learning gains.

- **Before- and after-school support programs:** Reserving time before or after school for math support can serve a small group of students who would benefit from targeted math instruction. However, the challenges to resolve are transportation and finding a competent tutor who communicates well with classroom teachers.

HYBRID LEADERSHIP TIPS

You'll want to work with math teachers whether your school is hybrid or all-virtual to improve students' knowledge of math operations and solving math word problems.

Use Formative Assessments

When students are virtual learners, teachers can assess them during class and after class office hours or while students work independently during the day. Teachers can assess hybrid students any time during the days they're at school.

Team Up With ELA Teachers

You need to coordinate and schedule times for math and ELA teachers to meet and collaborate on teaching students to solve word problems. You should attend these meetings as the facilitator and to deepen your understanding of the problem-solving process that both groups develop. Once teachers agree on a process, you can help them schedule time to team-teach virtually. However, with hybrid classes, either the math or the ELA teachers will execute the plans and then debrief.

Applying Intervention Strategies

Teachers can integrate any one of the eight intervention strategies starting on page 153, whether they're all-virtual or hybrid. Your role is to discuss the importance of being selective and choosing strategies that can benefit students. You'll also need to discuss with math teachers how they plan to document their interventions.

CONSIDER THESE ACTIONS AND AIM HIGH

- Discuss with math teachers the benefits of an asset model over a deficit model for improving students' math learning.

- Meet with your math department to learn to what extent teachers are helping students make math connections.

- Collaborate to discover how students learn to unpack and solve word problems.

- Organize a meeting of math and ELA teachers to explore how ELA teachers can increase students' understanding of the process for solving word problems.

- Have discussions with math teachers to explain the importance of deferring math placement tests and opening school by attending to students' emotional well-being and building trusting relationships.

- Develop with your math teachers some professional learning opportunities that can enable them to better differentiate instruction.

- Study the math intervention practices in your school and then collaborate with teachers to make these more effective for students.

- Form a group of math teachers to explore finding extra time in your school's schedule to support math learners for short or extended periods of time.

Closing Reminder

To show students the relevance of math to their lives, develop, with teachers, a math curriculum that invites students to apply math operation to word problems. In addition, encourage teachers to create interdisciplinary projects with colleagues that meet the needs of all learners, so students experience the connections between math and other subjects. Continually remind teachers to plan support lessons using "just in time teaching" and moving away from "just in case."

CHAPTER 8

Next Steps
Leading a Culture of Learning

Like me, I'm sure you're reflecting on collaborating with teachers to explore ways for students to adjust to school, and for you and teachers to increase emotional well-being. As you consider options that can work for your school, my recommendation is to ensure that your actions align with your school's mission and vision. Remember, as well, that discussions with faculty and staff should center on hope, developing trusting relationships, and sustaining a culture of learning that builds on students' strengths and responds to their needs.

THE PRINCIPAL: LEADER OF STUDENT SUCCESS

Schools that effectively transition out of the pandemic to all students attending school will need an involved, compassionate, and committed leader who values all community members and believes in an asset-based approach. Your words and actions should project these core beliefs: collaboration, shared teacher leadership, self- and collective efficacy, teacher and student agency, ongoing professional learning, and elevating students' learning gains.

GETTING STARTED WITH LITERACY AND NUMERACY INITIATIVES

When you recognize that you won't have all the answers when planning these initiatives, you'll seek ideas from teachers and other administrators and collaborate with them to develop a plan. Doing this shows how much you value their ideas and suggestions and also increase their investment in each initiative. Here are guidelines to get this rolling in your school and spark teachers' interest.

- Schedule two to four meetings with Math and ELA teachers.

- Principal, assistant principal, and other school leaders attend all meetings.

- Use information gathered to set two to three priorities to get started with the initiative. For example, you'll need professional learning on identified topics in math and literacy. Literacy teachers might develop an instructional reading unit that's differentiated, and math teachers might model how to read a two- and three-step word problem and suggest procedures for finding solutions.

- Meet and assess progress after two weeks and then after three weeks to determine supports needed and ways teachers can help one another.

Your top priority is to examine and evaluate agreed-upon suggestions, but expect that each initiative will not run smoothly. There will be bumps, roadblocks, and the need to collaborate to discuss and address them.

MOVING FORWARD WITH LITERACY AND NUMERACY INITIATIVES

As you and your team move forward, schedule additional meetings, and decide when you'll bring math and ELA teachers together. Here are guidelines to reflect on and adjust to your school's needs:

- Rank priorities unique to your school.

- Update professional learning topics.

- Periodically meet to assess progress. It there's a glitch prior to a meeting, encourage teachers to share with you and collaborate to find ways to resolve it. Possible example: A small group of students, skilled in computation, resist doing more practice at school and homework. Solution: Personalize learning for them using technology so they can apply their knowledge to problem solving in class, with a peer partner, and at home on their own.

Once both initiatives are steadily moving forward, it's time to collaborate with teachers to develop support strategies for planning units and for ongoing professional learning experiences.

MOVING FORWARD WITH INCREASING STUDENTS' LEARNING

The list that follows will support the importance of checking the progress of an initiative with the goal of celebrating progress and meeting to discuss challenges.

This isn't formal evaluation, but it's a way to enhance trusting relationships as well as teachers' self- and collective efficacy.

Co-planning units: Encourage teachers to work in pairs or small teams to develop literacy and numeracy units, as doing this encourages discussion, enables them to learn from one another, makes the process easier, honors professionalism, and continues to build positive relationships.

Peer observations: For that to occur, you'll need to discuss the benefits with teachers so they can learn from one another. To make this happen, it's helpful for you or another administrator to cover teachers' classes so they can observe a peer in action.

Teacher partnerships: Discuss with teachers the benefits of forming partnerships to informally discuss with you what's working and areas that require more attention. Moreover, partnerships encourage teachers to offer each other feedback that can improve instruction and students' learning.

Librarian's role: If your school has a librarian, that staffer can work closely with teachers to update them about new books in the collection as well as discuss ways to support students when they're in the library.

Follow-up conversations: You'll need to schedule these to ensure that teachers update you and that you also have opportunities to raise questions, discover their needs so you can provide assistance, and celebrate what's working.

Ongoing professional learning: When you and teachers develop literacy and numeracy initiatives, you'll need to collaborate to generate a list of topics that represent areas teachers want to study, discuss, and apply to their teaching.

AS YOU MOVE FORWARD, GIVE YOURSELF THE GIFT OF TIME

Since this book focuses on key elements of great leadership that are needed as students return to a normal school day, it's important to look back as you move forward. When schools closed in March 2020, fear of the unknown and the rapid changes in teaching and learning caused by COVID-19 left many school leaders and teachers feeling unprepared to meet the challenges of virtual and hybrid learning. Meaningful change takes time, especially when it includes collaborative discussions and reflection and strives to create a hopeful and optimistic community by intentionally elevating, inspiring, and empowering faculty and staff.

As I look back, I'm inspired by the way teachers and administrators met the needs of students. No one took a graduate course in "pandemic leadership," but it wasn't needed. What was needed and worked were the skills of excellent principals that can lead an entire school community through difficult challenges. Your leadership matters and makes a difference as you collaborate with teachers, students, and parents to create literacy and numeracy initiatives that increase all students' learning gains!

Appendix

STATION LEARNING

Station learning is an outstanding way to provide a group of students with the extra support they need while others work independently. For students working independently, you can use technology and have students watch a video on a topic related to a unit, or watch an instructional YouTube video, or read and respond to materials you provide. You can use station learning in English, math, history, and science classes.

PLANNING FORMAT

There are always three components to Station Learning Plans (see Figure A.1). At any time during a unit of study teachers can pause to support a group of students who would benefit from reteaching and extra practice. Take about fifteen minutes from instructional reading or math time for one to three consecutive days to support students by developing their understanding of a specific strategy such as: in math, two-step word problems, calculating percent; in English, inferring or comparing and contrasting. Then, organize two or more groups: students who complete enrichment and those who need some additional practice in order to internalize the learning. Ensure that directions are clear for groups working independently and encourage students to help one another. If you have a large class, you'll need multiple copies of materials so students can work in smaller groups. The form in Figure A.1 can be used to plan one to three lessons. For more detailed information and examples of what to include stations, go to https://catlintucker.com/2021/01/inspiration-station-rotation-lessons.

FIGURE A.1 ● Planning Form

TEACHER SUPPORTS A GROUP	STUDENTS WORK ON ENRICHMENT	STUDENTS COMPLETE EXTRA PRACTICE

LOOK-FOR CHECKLIST: TAKING YOUR SCHOOL'S COLLABORATIVE TEMPERATURE

Name _____ Position _____

Directions: Read the Look-For Checklist carefully and check statements that apply to your school. Collaborate to compare completed checklists and identify successes and needs.

Date Completed:	**Taking Your School's Collaborative Temperature**
_____	Teams and departments have collaborative discussions with school leaders.
_____	The principal or another school leader attends meetings that impact teachers and staff.
_____	The principal fosters teacher agency, empowering teachers to consider leadership opportunities.
_____	Teachers collaborate with school leaders on schoolwide initiatives.
_____	The principal collaborates with teachers and develops shared leadership opportunities.
_____	School leaders collaborate with staff on policies that affect them.
_____	The principal values teachers' input and feedback.
_____	Teams and departments collaborate to make shared decisions about curriculum and students' needs.

Additional Comments:

LOOK-FOR CHECKLIST: ASSESSING SCHOOLWIDE INITIATIVES

Name _____ Position _____

Directions: Read the Look-For Checklist carefully and check statements that apply to your school. Collaborate to compare completed checklists and identify successes and needs.

Date Completed:	Assessing Schoolwide Initiatives
_____	The principal guards against initiative overload.
_____	The principal schedules timely meetings to discuss an initiative.
_____	The principal collaborates with teachers to gather their feedback on possible new initiatives.
_____	The principal delegates specific jobs related to an initiative to teacher volunteers.
_____	The principal collaborates with teachers to develop methods for assessing the initiative's progress.
_____	Assessments of initiatives are frequent, making adjustments possible.
_____	The principal and other school leaders show through conversations and emails how much they value teachers' efforts regarding an initiative.

Additional Comments:

LOOK-FOR CHECKLIST: TAKING YOUR SCHOOL'S READING TEMPERATURE

Name _____ Position _____

Directions: Read the Look-For Checklist carefully and check statements that apply to your school. Collaborate to compare completed checklists and identify successes and needs.

Date Completed:	Taking Your School's Reading Temperature
_____	ELA classes have culturally relevant classroom libraries containing 500–600 books.
_____	Social studies, science, and math classes have classroom libraries with 200–250 books.
_____	The principal values independent reading and funds classroom libraries annually.
_____	Class schedules allow for fifteen to twenty minutes of independent reading of self-selected books each time class meets.
_____	ELA teachers use interactive read-alouds as a teaching tool to show students how they apply strategies and respond to diverse texts.
_____	Teachers in ELA and content classes read aloud every time class meets to enhance students' knowledge of genres, topics, and pleasure in listening to texts.
_____	The principal reads aloud to different classes.
_____	The librarian helps teachers select culturally relevant books.
_____	The librarian updates teachers on new additions to the media center.
_____	School leaders, teachers, and staff list books they're presently reading and post titles and authors on their doors.

(Continued)

_____ Students select an independent reading book and present book talks to their classes about once a month.

_____ Bulletin boards in hallways have student work that celebrates reading.

_____ Students write about reading in their notebooks.

_____ Books used for instruction include culturally relevant titles.

_____ Instructional reading units organized by genre and/or theme differentiate students' reading choices.

_____ The principal lets parents know the importance of independent reading at home.

_____ Teachers explain to parents how independent reading improves students' skill, explaining why it's important for students to read at home.

_____ Homework in ELA classes asks students to read a self-selected book for twenty to thirty minutes each evening.

_____ Students keep a record of their independent reading by recording the title and author of a book and the date they completed or abandoned the book.

_____ Teachers model how they write responses to reading in their notebooks.

Additional Comments:

15 BENEFITS OF INDEPENDENT READING

"A book is a dream you hold in your hand." —Neil Gaiman

1. Refines students' understanding of applying strategies, for during independent reading, students have multiple opportunities to practice what they learn during instructional reading.

2. Develops an understanding of how diverse genres work as readers figure out the likenesses and differences among realistic, historical, and science fiction, fantasy, mystery, thrillers, biography, memoir, informational texts, and so on.

3. Enlarges background knowledge and deepens readers' understanding of people as they get to know different characters.

4. Builds vocabulary as students meet and understand words in diverse contexts. Independent reading, not vocabulary workbooks, is the best way to enlarge vocabulary because students meet words in the context of their reading.

5. Teaches students how to self-select "good fit" books they can and want to read.

6. Develops students' agency and literary tastes. Choice builds agency, and as students choose and dip into diverse genres and topics, they discover the types of books they enjoy.

7. Strengthens reading stamina, their ability to focus on reading for twenty minutes to one hour.

8. Improves silent reading. Through daily practice students develop their in-the-head reading voice and learn to read in meaningful phrases.

9. Develops reading fluency because of the practice that voluminous reading offers.

10. Supports recall of information learners need as they read long texts that ask them to hold details presented in early chapters in their memory so they can access them later in the book.

11. Improves reading rate through the practice that volume provides.

12. Develops students' imagination as they visualize settings, what characters and people look like, conflicts, decisions, problems, interactions, and so forth.

13. Fosters the enjoyment of visual literacy when students read picture books and graphic texts.

14. Creates empathy for others as students learn to step into the skin of characters and experience their lives.

15. Transfers a passion for reading to students' outside-of-school lives and develops the volume in reading students need to become proficient and advanced readers.

A DEEPER DIVE INTO FIVE MATH INTERVENTIONS THAT MATTER!

These five math interventions invite teachers to differentiate instruction and meet the needs of students below, on, and above grade-level expectations. Teachers can find, watch, and discuss YouTube videos on all of these math strategies.

MATH THINK-ALOUDS AND COLD WRITES

Think-alouds ask teachers to talk out loud and show students their thinking process as they complete specific math operations and solve word problems. So students can observe and listen to think-alouds, teachers need a document camera and math notebook as they write and talk, cross out and revise their math work, and then field questions from students. This powerful learning strategy builds and enlarges students' mental model of a math process, and the completed written solution becomes a resource that students can review by rereading and that the teacher can use to reteach.

GUIDED MATH GROUPS

Guided math groups allow teachers to support all learners in their class. Start by reviewing a set of formative assessments to organize students into three groups: those who need intervention and reteaching, those who require some extra practice before moving on, and students who are ready for enrichment. Groups meet for no more than fifteen minutes, and when teachers work with one group, other groups can work independently and watch a video or use technology for practice or enrichment. The benefit of guided math groups is that teachers work with all students, not just those who require intervention.

Students in Grades K–4 might experience guided math groups throughout the year. In Grades 5 and up, with departmentalized schedules, guided-practice math groups can meet a few times over one to two weeks.

CHOICE BOARDS

Choice boards can be implemented at any grade level and include a wide range of learning experiences at varying levels of difficulty. Students can complete the activities by working in pairs, small groups, or independently. Post the choice board and explain each activity, so students know what to do and where to find their materials—online or a designated place in the classroom. Then circulate among students to explain the directions for specific choices, so they know expectations and can ask questions. Continue circulating and monitor students' work so all have success and improve. Another benefit of choice boards is that modifications of some choices can be made for inclusion and teachers can integrate them seamlessly onto the grid of choices. The challenge to teachers developing choice boards is to develop meaningful math lessons that are accessible to all students in their classes.

PERSONALIZED LEARNING

Personalized learning customizes students' math learning experiences according to students' unique skills, preferences, and prior math experiences. Teachers invite students to learn at their own pace, allowing them to steadily move forward as teachers use adaptive math software to adjust to each student's needs. It can also include math projects that individual students work on using a combination of software, videos, and online research. Personalized learning is labor intensive for teachers and requires them to select appropriate tech to develop learning plans. Teachers can use it to differentiate for enrichment and extra practice, or they can decide to personalize learning for all students during a two- to three-week mini-unit or project.

BLENDED LEARNING

The main idea behind blended learning is that some students learn better with a combination of digital experiences and face-to-face learning with a teacher and/or peers. Students have more choices and flexibility with blended learning because they're in control of deciding or negotiating with teachers their digital experiences. In large classes that have students with a wide range of math skill, blended learning can free teachers to support students who require intervention while others work independently using technology or solve problems with peers and meet with teachers during brief conferences to ensure that they are progressing.

READING LOG

Title, Author	Date Finished/Abandoned

References

CHAPTER 1

Australian Institute for Teaching and School Leadership. (2019). *Australian professional standard for principals and the leadership profiles.* Melbourne, Australia: Author. https://www.aitsl.edu.au/docs/default-source/national-policy-framework/australian-professional-standard-for-principals-and-the-leadership-profiles-(web).pdf

Blasé, J., & Blasé, J. (1999). Principals' instructional leadership and teacher development: Teachers' perspectives. *Educational Administration Quarterly, 35*(3), 349–378.

Cotton, K. (2003). *Principals and student achievement: What the research says.* Alexandria, VA: Association for Supervision and Curriculum Development.

DuFour, R., DuFour, R., Eaker, R., & Many, T. (2010). *Learning by doing: A handbook for professional learning communities at work.* Bloomington, IN: Solution Tree Press.

Hallinger, P. (2005). Instructional leadership and the school principal: A passing fancy that refuses to fade away. *Leadership and Policy in Schools, 4*(3), 221–239. https://doi.org/10.1080/15700760500244793

Hargreaves, A., & Fink, D. (2003). Sustaining leadership. *Phi Delta Kappan, 84*(9), 693–700. https://doi.org/10.1177/003172170308400910

Leithwood, A., & Riel, C. (2003). *What do we already know about successful school leadership?* Washington, DC: AERA Division A Task Force on Developing Research in Educational Leadership.

Marzano, R. J., Waters, T., & McNulty, B. A. (2005). *School leadership that works.* Denver, CO: McRel.

Portin, B., Schneider, P., DeArmond, M., & Gundlach, L. (2003). *Making sense of leading schools: A study of the school principalship.* Seattle, WA: Center on Reinventing Public Education.

CHAPTER 2

Fairman, J. C., & Mackenzie, S. V. (2012). Spheres of teacher leadership action for learning. *Professional Development in Education, 38*(2), 229–246.

Hattie, J. A. C. (2015). *What works in education: The politics of collaborative expertise.* London, UK: Pearson.

Mendel, C. M., Watson, R. L., & MacGregor, C. J. (2002). *A study of leadership behaviors of elementary principals compared with school culture* [Paper presentation]. Southern Regional Council for Educational Administration, Kansas City, MO.

Senge, P. (1994). *The fifth discipline fieldbook.* New York: Doubleday.

Spillane, J. P., Halverson, R., & Diamond, J. B. (2004). Towards a theory of leadership practice: A distributed perspective. *Journal of Curriculum Studies, 36*(1), 3–34.

CHAPTER 3

Allington, R. L., & Johnston, P. H. (2002). *Reading to learn: Lessons from exemplary fourth-grade classrooms.* New York, NY: Guilford Press.

Covey, S. M. R., & Merrill, R. R. (2006). *The speed of trust: The one thing that changes everything.* New York, NY: Free Press.

Howard, J. R., Milner-McCall, T., & Howard, T. C. (2020). *No more teaching without positive relationships.* Portsmouth, NH: Heinemann.

Robb, L., & Robb, E. (2019). *TeamMakers: Positively impacting the lives of children through district-wide dreaming, collaborating, and change.* San Diego, CA: Burgess Publishing.

Schaps, E. (2003). Creating a school community. *Educational Leadership, 60*(6), 31–33. http://www.ascd.org/publications/educational-leadership/mar03/vol60/num06/Creating-a-School-Community.aspx

Tschannen-Moran, M. (2004). *Trust matters: Leadership for successful schools.* San Francisco, CA: Jossey-Bass.

CHAPTER 4

Ashton, P. T., & Webb, R. B. (1986). *Making a difference: Teachers' sense of efficacy and student achievement.* New York, NY: Longman.

Eells, R. (2011). *Meta-analysis of the relationship between collective teacher efficacy and student achievement* (Doctoral dissertation, Loyola University Chicago). Dissertations, Paper No. 133. http://ecommons.luc.edu/luc_diss/133

CHAPTER 5

Allington, R. L. (2007). Intervention all day long: New hope for struggling readers. *Voices from the Middle, 14*(4), 7–14.

ASCD. On savage inequalities: A conversation with Jonathan Kozol. *Educational Leadership.* https://www.ascd.org/publications/educational-leadership/dec92/vol50/num04/On-Savage-Inequalities@-A-Conversation-with-Jonathan-Kozol.aspx 4.

Blasé, J., & Kirby, P. C. (2000). *Bringing out the best in teachers: What effective principals do* (2nd ed.). Thousand Oaks, CA: Corwin Press.

Donohoo, J., Hattie, J., & Eells, R. (2018). The power of collective efficacy. *Educational Leadership, 75*(6).

Hoy, W. K., Sweetland, S. R., & Smith, P. A. (2002). Toward an organizational model of achievement in high schools: The significance of collective efficacy. *Educational Administration Quarterly, 38*(1), 77–93. https://doi.org/10.1177/0013161X02381004

ILA (2020). What's hot in literacy instruction? https://ila.online library.wiley.com/doi/full/10.1002/trtr.1904

Lambert, L. (2003). *Leadership capacity for lasting school improvement.* Alexandria, VA: Association for Supervision and Curriculum Development.

Miller, J. J. (2020). *The student-centred classroom: Transforming your teaching and grading practices.* Bloomington, IN: Solution Tree Press.

Neuman, S. B., & Moland, N. (2019). Book deserts: The consequences of income segregation on children's access to print. *Urban Education, 54*(1), 126–147. https://doi.org/10.1177/0042085916654525

Quintero, E. (2014, April 30). We can't just raise expectations. Reprinted in *The Washington Post* from the Albert Shanker Institute Blog.

Robb, L. (2016). *Differentiating reading instruction: How to teach reading to meet the needs of each student.* New York, NY: Scholastic.

Robb, L. (2017). *Read, talk, write: 35 lessons that teach students to analyze fiction and nonfiction.* Thousand Oaks, CA: Corwin Literacy.

Robb, L. (2022). *Teaching to increase volume in reading.* Champaign, IL: NCTE.

Sims Bishop, R. (1990). Mirrors, windows, and sliding glass doors. *Perspectives, 1*(3), ix–xi.

Tomlinson, C. A. (2017). *How to differentiate instruction in academically diverse classrooms* (3rd ed.). Alexandria, VA: ASCD.

CHAPTER 6

Babbitt, N. (1975). *Tuck everlasting.* New York, NY: Square Fish.

Fountas, I. C., & Pinnell, G. S. (2009). *Benchmark assessment system.* Portsmouth, NH: Heinemann.

Graham, S., & Hebert, M. (2010). *Writing to read: Evidence for how writing can improve reading.* New York, NY: The Carnegie Corporation.

Graham, S., Perrin, K. R., & Santangelo, T. (2015). Research-based writing practices and the common core: Meta-analysis and meta-synthesis. *The Elementary School Journal, 115,* 498–522.

Johnson, M. M. (2017). Assigning more writing—with less grading. *Edutopia, George Lucas Educational Foundation.* Retrieved September 26, 2017, from https://www.edutopia.org/article/assigning-more-writing-less-grading

Robb, L. (2017). *Read, talk, write: 35 lessons that teach students to analyze fiction and nonfiction.* Thousand Oaks, CA: Corwin Literacy.

Robb, L. (2022). *Teaching reading to increase volume.* Champaign, IL: NCTE.

Robb, L., & Robb, E. (2020). *Schools full of readers: Tools for teachers, coaches, and leaders to support students*. New Rochelle, NY: Benchmark Education.

Robb, L., Goldberg, G., & Houser, R. (2020). *The power of independent reading: Developing readers who can read and want to read, a white paper*. Portsmouth, NH: Stenhouse Publishers.

Yates, K., & Nosek, C. (2018). *To know and nurture a reader: Conferring with confidence and joy*. Portland, ME: Stenhouse Publishers.

CHAPTER 7

Council of the Great City Schools. (2020). Addressing unfinished learning after COVID-19 school closures. https://www.cgcs.org/cms/lib/DC00001581/Centricity/Domain/313/CGCS_Unfinished%20Learning.pdf

Drake, S. M., & Burns, R. C. (2004). *Meeting standards through integrated curriculum*. Alexandria, VA: ASCD.

Fensterwald, J. (2020). Early data on learning loss show big drop in math, but not reading skills. *EdSource*. https://edsource.org/2020/early-data-on-learning-loss-show-big-drop-in-math-but-not-reading-skills/644416

Pearce, K. (2018). *The complete guide to spiralling your math curriculum*. https://tapintoteenminds.com/spiralling-guide/

Pearson, P. D., & Gallagher, M. C. (1983). The instruction of reading comprehension. *Contemporary Educational Psychology*, 8(3), 317–344. https://doi.org/10.1016/0361-476X(83)90019-X

Sammons, L., & Boucher, D. (2017). *Guided math workshop: Successfully plan, organize, implement and manage guided math workshops in K-8th grade classrooms*. Huntington Beach, CA: Shell Education.

Vigotsky, L. S. (1978). *Mind in society: The development of higher psychological processes*. Cambridge, MA: Harvard University Press.

Index

Leadership That Makes an Impact

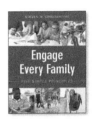

PETER M. DEWITT

This step-by-step how-to guide presents the six driving forces of instructional leadership within a multistage model for implementation, delivering lasting improvement through small collaborative changes.

JOHN HATTIE & RAYMOND L. SMITH

Based on the most current Visible Learning® research with contributions from education thought leaders around the world, this book includes practical ideas for leaders to implement high-impact strategies to strengthen entire school cultures and advocate for all students.

DOUGLAS FISHER, NANCY FREY, DOMINIQUE SMITH, & JOHN HATTIE

This essential hands-on resource offers guidance on leading school and school systems from a distance and delivering on the promise of equitable, quality learning experiences for students.

STEVEN M. CONSTANTINO

Explore the how-to's of establishing family empowerment through building trust, and reflect on implicit bias, equitable learning outcomes, and the role family engagement plays.

MICHAEL FULLAN, JOANNE QUINN, & JOANNE MCEACHEN

The comprehensive strategy of deep learning incorporates practical tools and processes to engage educational stakeholders in new partnerships, mobilize whole-system change, and transform learning for all students.

JOANNE QUINN, JOANNE MCEACHEN, MICHAEL FULLAN, MAG GARDNER, & MAX DRUMMY

Dive into deep learning with this hands-on guide to creating learning experiences that give purpose, unleash student potential, and transform not only learning, but life itself.

DAVIS CAMPBELL & MICHAEL FULLAN

The model outlined in this book develops a systems approach to governing local schools collaboratively to become exemplars of highly effective decision making, leadership, and action.

DAVIS CAMPBELL, MICHAEL FULLAN, BABS KAVANAUGH, & ELEANOR ADAM

As a supplement to the best-selling *The Governance Core*, this guide will help trustees and superintendents adopt a governance mindset and cohesive partnership.

To order your copies, visit **corwin.com/leadership**

**SIMON BREAKSPEAR &
BRONWYN RYRIE JONES**
Realistic in demand and innovative in approach, this practical and powerful improvement process is designed to help all teachers get going, and keep going, with incremental professional improvement in schools.

**JAMES BAILEY &
RANDY WEINER**
The thought-provoking daily reflections in this guided journal are designed to strengthen the social and emotional skills of leaders and create a strong social-emotional environment for leaders, teachers, and students.

**MARK WHITE &
DWIGHT L. CARTER**
Through understanding the past and envisioning the future, the authors use practical exercises and real-life examples to draw the blueprint for adapting schools to the age of hyper-change.

**ALLAN G. OSBORNE, JR.
& CHARLES J. RUSSO**
With its user-friendly format, this resource will help educators understand the law so they can focus on providing exemplary education to students.

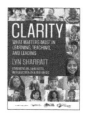

**MICHAEL FULLAN &
MARY JEAN GALLAGHER**
With the goal of transforming the culture of learning to develop greater equity, excellence, and student well-being, this book will help you liberate the system and maintain focus.

**TOM VANDER ARK
& EMILY LIEBTAG**
Diverse case studies and a framework based on timely issues help educators focus students' talents and interests on developing an entrepreneurial mindset and leadership skills.

THOMAS HATCH
By highlighting what works and demonstrating what can be accomplished if we redefine conventional schools, we can have more efficient, more effective, and more equitable schools and create powerful opportunities to support all aspects of students' development.

LYN SHARRATT
Explore 14 essential parameters to guide system and school leaders toward building powerful collaborative learning cultures.

A SAGE Publishing Company

CORWIN HAS ONE MISSION: to enhance education through intentional professional learning.

We build long-term relationships with our authors, educators, clients, and associations who partner with us to develop and continuously improve the best evidence-based practices that establish and support lifelong learning.